ARMED TO RESIST!

PALMETTO
PUBLISHING
Charleston, SC
www.PalmettoPublishing.com

Armed to Resist!
Copyright © 2023 by Stephanie Jaworski

To contact the author please TEXT "Armed to Resist" at 608-480-3330.

Hardcover ISBN: 979-8-8229-3307-1
Paperback ISBN: 979-8-8229-1964-8

ARMED to RESIST!

Remaining faithful to the Word of God in the hour of apostasy

STEPHANIE JAWORSKI

Table of Contents

Introduction

Today, there is a remnant wondering what Christianity has become. While secularization trends have accelerated over the past few decades, the power of faith, which was once a fundamental pillar of the Christian life, has undergone a noticeable decline in recent times. This shift can be attributed to a growing attempt to maintain cultural relevance; many modern churches have redefined the historic Christian faith by turning away from the teachings of the Bible. This has generated skepticism among followers as they witness a divergence from the core principles of truth and sincerity. These misguided practices not only tarnish the reputation of The Church of Jesus Christ but also contribute to the waning influence of faith in people's lives.

In these uncertain times, it's easy to become disheartened by the changes we witness around us. Yet, history has shown that it's during such periods of spiritual dryness that humanity often experiences some of its most profound awakenings. Just as a caterpillar must undergo a transformative process within its cocoon to emerge as a butterfly, so must our faith undergo its metamorphosis to reach new heights of understanding and relevance. Just as a crisis can be a turning point that transforms adversity into opportunity, our challenges can push us to reevaluate our beliefs and open new paths of understanding.

This beckons us to lift our gaze beyond the mundane and fleeting, fixing our eyes on the promises of heaven. As Psalm 121:1-2 says, "I lift up my eyes to the hills. From where does my help come? My help comes from the Lord, who made heaven and earth." By embracing the teaching of the bible, we, those who seek Truth, can rekindle the fire of our calling, becoming beacons of light that pierce through the darkness of despair.

As we embark on this exploration of the future of religion, let us do so with a sense of optimism and curiosity. Let us embrace the unknown with open hearts, for it is in the unknown that we often discover the true extent of our potential. Just as explorers once set sail to discover new worlds, we too are setting forth on a voyage of discovery—one that will not only shed light on the future of Christianity in the nation but also illuminate the boundless capacity of the human spirit to endure, adapt, and thrive.

In the chapters that follow, we will delve deeper into how to redefine Christian faith for cultural relevance and call for churches to return to fundamental Bible teachings. We will address the societal shift from objective truth to moral relativism and emphasize the importance of holding onto the unchanging truths found in the Bible. Just as Proverbs 3:5-6 reminds us, "Trust in the Lord with all your heart, and do not lean on your own understanding. In all your ways, acknowledge him, and he will make straight your paths."

Also, we will explore the concepts of forgiveness and letting go of grudges, drawing inspiration from passages like Matthew 6:14-15: "For if you forgive others their trespasses, your heavenly Father will also forgive you, but if you do not forgive others their trespasses, neither will your Father forgive your trespasses." Additionally, we will discuss the importance of submitting to God's process of change, as Jeremiah 29:11 declares, "For I know the plans I have for you, declares the Lord, plans for welfare and not for evil, to give you a future and a hope."

We will talk about how to focus on personal growth rather than manipulating God. We will uncover the wisdom of passages like Philippians 2:12-13: "Therefore, my beloved, as you have always obeyed, so now, not only as in my presence but much more in my absence, work out your own salvation with fear and trembling, for it is God who works in you, both to will and to work for his good pleasure."

In addition, we will explore how to understand the upside-down nature of the Kingdom, inspired by Jesus' teachings in the Beatitudes (Matthew 5:3-12). We will discuss how to pursue Jesus relentlessly, even though difficulties, echoing Paul's words in Philippians 3:14, "I press on toward the goal for the prize of the upward call of God in Christ Jesus."

We will also explore how to prioritize God's will over personal desires; we will draw inspiration from Jesus' example in the Garden of Gethsemane, as he prayed, "Father, if you are willing, remove this cup from me. Nevertheless, not my will, but yours, be done" (Luke 22:42).

As we embark on this transformative journey through the chapters ahead, brace yourself for eye-opening insights that challenge the status quo and empower you to champion a revival of authentic Christian values in an ever-evolving world. The call to action is clear: it's time to embrace the timeless wisdom of the Bible, unravel the complexities of our changing society, and forge an unbreakable connection with the divine. Get ready to revolutionize your perspective, ignite your faith, and set your course towards a future where unwavering devotion to God's truth reignites the world with purpose and meaning. Your faith's next chapter starts now – are you ready to embrace the challenge?

Chapter 1

THE TREND IN MODERN CHURCH

From its origins in the teachings of Jesus Christ to its diverse manifestations in the present day, the church has undergone numerous transformations that reflect the evolving nature of human society and spirituality. In the modern era, the church is experiencing yet another trend that is shaping its character and influence. This trend, characterized by shifts in theology, worship styles, and outreach efforts, is redefining the role of the church in the lives of individuals and communities.

The decline in biblical literacy is not solely a result of societal changes. The evolving approach of certain churches towards biblical interpretation plays a pivotal role. It is crucial for churches to reexamine their methods and align themselves with the true foundation set by God, as emphasized in 1 Corinthians 3:9-15.

The apostle Paul, in his first letter to the Corinthians, highlighted the importance of building on God's foundation. He wrote, "For we are God's fellow workers. You are God's field, God's building. According to the grace of God given to me, like a skilled master builder, I laid a foundation, and someone else is building upon it. Let each one take care of how he builds upon it. For no one can lay a foundation other than that which is laid, which is Jesus Christ. Now, if anyone builds on the foundation with gold, silver, precious stones, wood, hay, or straw—each one's work will become manifest, for the day will disclose it, because it will be revealed by fire, and the fire will test what sort of work each one has done. If the work that anyone has built on the foundation survives, he will receive a reward. If anyone's work is burned up, he will suffer loss, though he himself will be saved, but only as through fire." (1 Cor 3:9-15). This Bible verse beautifully encapsulates the concept that the Church is not merely an institution but a divine construct with God as its ultimate architect. Just as any skilled builder lays the foundation first, Paul's words remind us of the necessity to establish our faith and understanding on God's Word.

Some churches have drifted away from this foundational principle. They have strayed into interpreting the Bible in ways that align more with human desires and societal trends rather than adhering to the true teachings of Scripture. This departure has led to the weakening of the spiritual foundation of these congregations, causing a disconnection from the core messages of the Bible.

Paul's warning in 1 Corinthians 3:10-11 serves as a reminder that any attempt to build on a foundation other than Christ is futile. When churches prioritize human doctrines and trends over the unchanging Word of God, they risk erecting structures that lack the stability and endurance required to weather the storms of life.

Paul goes on to explain the consequences of building on such faulty foundations. In 1 Corinthians 3:12-13, he states, "Now if anyone builds on the foundation with gold, silver, precious stones, wood, hay, straw—each one's work will become manifest, for the Day will disclose it, because it will be revealed by fire, and the fire will test what sort of work each one has done" (ESV). The imagery of fire testing the quality of the materials used in construction emphasizes the importance of using lasting and valuable components in our spiritual edifice.

For churches to rekindle biblical literacy and strengthen their foundation, they must prioritize the timeless truths of Scripture above fleeting ideologies, psycology, financial coaching and self-centered preaching. Just as the psalmist meditates on God's law day and night (Psalm 1:2), believers should immerse themselves in the Word to discern God's will and develop a deeper understanding of His teachings. The act of meditating on Scripture allows for a more profound connection with the divine wisdom that guides our lives.

Churches should encourage their members to follow the example of the noble Bereans, who "received the word with all eagerness, examining the Scriptures daily to see if these things were so" (Acts 17:11, ESV). This diligent pursuit of truth ensures that the foundations of faith remain steadfast, resisting the erosion of false teachings and worldly influences.

It is said in the Bible that God came to visit Adam in the cool of the day in a garden. I imagine that the Lord was walking through the garden and he would come to sit and talk with Adam. I believe that wasn't just once. It was a habit, maybe a special rendez-vous that they had. And today in churches, yet I still hear: "Lord visit us! Come touch us"! And we beg, we beg, over and over! But that is "garden mentality"! Let me submit to you that we're not in the garden anymore. The Lord Jesus came and died a painful death on the cross, resurrected and sent us the Holy Spirit to dwell in us! He just doesn't want to come visit. He wants to come dwell.

If you have a house and you ever had an apartment, I'm sure that you don't come and visit your home, you come to dwell in it. You come to stay in your home. This present generation go around and say: "oh, I need a touch from God, a visitation from him". And we are all about the experience and the goosebumps and the big shouts, all lock up in "a feeling". Yet the Lord desires to bring His Church forth to another level.

God, used to also visit Abraham and Moses. Until one day things started to change. There was now a tabernacle, a tent of meeting. Notice the evolution here. First, God is coming to visit Adam in the garden, then He visits Moses face to face, later in the wilderness God comes and lives with the people of Israel. He lived with them in a tent.

Later, after they entered the promise land, in the times of David, he came and lived with them as well. Wherever the Ark of the Covenant was, there the presence of God was. But now Jesus comes, and He introduce yet another reality. We go from God visiting, to God living with, to the God who live inside. The God who dells in us. He came and made it about tearing up the veil of separation so that He can enter a live inside of his People.

Philippians 2:11 says "this mind be in You, which also in Christ Jesus, who being in the form of God thought it not robbery to be equal with God but made himself of no reputation and took upon him the form of a servant and was made in the likeness of man and being found in fashion as a man." And the powerful verse goes on to say: "He humbled himself. Became obedient unto death. Even the death of the cross, God wherefore, also has highly exalted him and given him a name which is above every name, that at the name of Jesus, every knee will bow of things in heaven and things on earth, and things under the earth. And that every tongue should confess that Jesus Christ is Lord to the glory of God the Father".

The church needs to abandon all its self-centered gospel. Jesus didn't have that high exaltation by coming on earth and campaigning for himself. He came and lived 30 years in complete darkness. He lived completely anonymous on the earth. For 30 years, God made in flesh was on earth and did, well according to the bible, nothing. He waited 30 years to start his ministry. People thought that it was going to come as the Messiah, that they were expecting to come and take over! They were expecting The Messiah to come and impose a political reformation. But that was not the will of the Father. He came, fulfill the will of the Father, and he was obedience to the point of death.

Chapter 2

THE NEED TO REVERSE THE TREND

The Bible itself emphasizes the significance of knowing and internalizing its teachings. In the book of Hosea, the prophet conveys God's desire for His people to have knowledge of Him: "My people are destroyed for lack of knowledge; because you have rejected knowledge, I reject you from being a priest to me" (Hosea 4:6, ESV). This poignant verse underscores the consequences of neglecting God's Word and highlights the vital role that knowledge plays in our spiritual lives.

Today, we go to church, and we hear a lot about the things of God, and we hear about Him. Do we get it though? Are we able to walk it out? You hear those things over and over again. Unless we apply it in our personal life, we will not bear fruits. The fruits of the Spirit are what we need to walk in the fullness of who we are in Him. But first the word of God need to become a revelation. A revelation is the Holy Spirit in us putting the teaching of the bible in the light of our personal walk. Not anyone else! So let us work and work relentlessly toward applying every aspect of the word of God in our

Lives. He is the Word. And the word has to be in us, working in us to make us perfect until His return!

There is a coming together in agreement with The Word of God, that need to take place in my spirit, so that I can manifest the Kingdom. If I get busy working on me, I won't have time to point the finger at anyone else. Fellowshipping with Jesus means to apply His word. No wander He said, "If you love me, keep and obey My Commandments!" John 14:15-24.

To reverse the trend of declining biblical literacy, individuals and churches must take intentional steps to prioritize the study and application of Scripture. The apostle Paul's exhortation to Timothy serves as a guiding light: "Do your best to present yourself to God as one approved, a worker who has no need to be ashamed, rightly handling the word of truth" (2 Timothy 2:15, ESV). This verse encapsulates the idea that understanding the Word requires effort and diligence. Just as a skilled craftsman takes care in their work, believers should approach the study of the Bible with dedication and a desire to comprehend its deeper meanings.

The Psalms echo the joy and fulfillment that come from immersing oneself in God's Word. "Blessed is the man who walks not in the counsel of the wicked, nor stands in the way of sinners, nor sits in the seat of scoffers; but his delight is in the law of the Lord, and on his law he meditates day and night" (Psalm 1:1-2, ESV). This imagery of delighting in God's law and meditating on it day and night paints a picture of a thriving spiritual life nurtured by the regular consumption of Scripture.

True followers of Jesus Christ have a significant role to play in reversing the trend of declining biblical literacy in today's churches. The apostle Paul's words to the Romans emphasize the power of God's Word to transform lives: "Do not be conformed to this world, but be transformed by the renewal of your mind, that by testing you may discern what the will of God is, what is good and acceptable and perfect" (Romans 12:2, ESV). Churches should actively engage their congregations in deepening their understanding of Scripture, helping them discern God's will amid the noise of the world.

You know in the Old Testament the altar was where the things of the flesh, was deposited. As a sacrifice the animal was put on the altar, it was for the flesh to be consumed until the point of ashes. See, the brazen altar was not a BBQ pit! It was an altar in which the flesh was to be burnt up until incinerated and reduced to ash.

The problem with us, Christian of today is that when we put our flesh on the altar, we don't wait until it completely dies, burnt up and incinerated by the fire of God. When the fire becomes too hot, we kick, we scream, and we want out. We like to pacify ourselves with the water down gospel preached in popular churches. Or we simply make convenient decision to orient our lives away from the inconvenience of the price to pay to be called by the Name of our Lord Jesus Christ.

Chapter 3

THE CHRISTIAN'S CALL TO CONVICTION

The present altar in a New Testament, the new level, the upgraded version of the brazing altar is the cross. We excel at telling him how beautiful He is. How strong and mighty He can be. We are quite good, for some of us, at casting devils out and using His given authority. But when He wants to come in our life as the God who cleanse us, break, and reshape our character we suddenly become a bit hesitant to answer present. He wants to crucify our bad habits and our flows on the cross.

Church grab your pride, offer it up as a living sacrifice and make sure that you leave it on the alter until it becomes ashes! Do not go back and when the pride is but only half cooked, we decide we want to pick it back again and go about our business. Church of the Living God! do not be distracted by church programs and potluck Sundays, forget not the way to His presence by prayers and supplications! Only the latter will wash your spots and your wrinkles out of your garment before His dreaded return.

Our agenda, our will, our wicked hearts as the bible so truthfully calls it in Jeremiah 17:9, should not only be cooked thoroughly. No that is not enough! We do not get to decide to jump out of the process because it hurts. If we know Him as Lord, we will submit until His work is finished. Our flesh should be incinerated and reduced to ashes. You know what they would do with those ashes back in the Old Testament? They would take the ashes and they would clean all the instruments and objects dedicated to the service of God!

If we want to do ministry, acceptable service to God, acceptable worship, acceptable adoration, we need to let the flesh become ashes. If we don't, eventually what happened is that we will find ourselves staying and hanging out in the outer court. We will not fully come in because flesh cannot go into the presence of God. We will start feeling stagnant in God. Dry and in need of a new thing. That is why many Christians go from churches to the next in quest of another "encounter". Don't become a spiritual vagabond! If you feel that something is resisting, you check and apply the word of God to your own walk and your own character. Seek The Lord's mercy to comprehend His Word and reveal to you what is keeping you from going deeper.

Church of The Living God, come back to authenticity. Authenticity in the Lord Jesus Christ. Running away from the responsibility of dealing with our fallen nature makes us spiritual coward!

We will never know how to forgive somebody if no one hurts us! Forgiveness hurts! It is costly. It cost our Lord Jesus everything! If you are in your comfort zone and you strive to make sure everyone loves and approve of you. You work very hard on your outward reality, so nobody comes to humiliate you. Because you are scared to be ruffled. Some of us become paranoid about every relationship in church and between brother and sister and we develop an imposter syndrome. We don't even have a pure heart anymore. We always have a double agenda. An imposter cannot worship in spirit and in truth! Come as you are, and The King of Glory will lift your head!

The story of David and Goliath also serves as a testament to the courage that stems from strong convictions. As a young shepherd, David faced the towering giant with unwavering faith in God's might. His audacious belief that God would deliver him enabled him to triumph against all odds. This biblical narrative illustrates that when Christians stand firm in their convictions, they are armed with an indomitable strength.

When Christians unflinchingly uphold their authenticity, they inspire others to seek truth, embrace love, and find solace in faith. Each bold action taken to shine a light serves as a ripple that can lead to waves of change.

Imagine a world where every believer steps out in boldness, extending a helping hand to the needy, offering comfort to the brokenhearted, and spreading kindness to the forgotten. Such actions create a chain reaction of compassion and hope, illuminating the darkest corners of society. Martin Luther King Jr., an emblem of conviction, proclaimed, "Darkness cannot drive out darkness; only light can do that. Hate cannot drive out hate; only love can do that." This sentiment echoes the essence of a Christian's role in the world—to be agents of light and love.

The Bible provides an arsenal of verses that empower believers to stand unwaveringly in their convictions. In Matthew 5:14-16, Jesus exhorts, "You are the light of the world. Let your light shine before others, that they may see your good deeds and glorify your Father in heaven." This divine charge encourages Christians to be a radiant testimony to God's goodness and grace.

Proverbs 3:5-6 reminds believers to trust in the Lord with all their hearts and lean not on their understanding. This verse exemplifies the need for faith and conviction even when circumstances appear daunting. When Christians fully rely on God's wisdom, their boldness becomes a beacon that guides them through life's challenges.

In times of doubt, believers can take refuge in Isaiah 41:10, where God promises, "Fear not, for I am with you; be not dismayed, for I am your God; I will strengthen you, I will help you, I will uphold you with my righteous right hand." This assurance serves as a powerful reminder that God's presence and strength sustain those who step out in faith.

Ultimately, the call to be bold in convictions and shine one's light is a transformative journey that impacts not only individual lives but the world at large. Each act of courage, each expression of faith, contributes to the tapestry of change, illuminating the darkness and revealing the beauty of God's truth.

One of my songs in my album is the Crucify King. When the Lord gave me that song, he said: "Watch and see that this song will become a hymn for the remnant of my people, those who truly understand what type of King I AM." We serve a king that has been crucified. Our allegiance goes to that guy who came from the other dimension, all powerful God who put himself in the little body, suppressing all His powers and abilities. He came to be obedient to His father until the point of death. Not any little death, but the death of the cross. He didn't take himself off the cross, nor did he say "OK, that's enough, that hurts too much. I guess I am going to call it off now father!"

Jesus, our Lord, didn't say "okay, I'm about to, I'm just about to die. So, I'm done now. I'm almost died for humanity." He was crucified. And the amount of sufferance inflicted by the cross was crucially painful. Faith in the Father was enough the endure this fate. Faith that the father will raise Him up on the third day. His was at peace during the process because He knew it was the Will of God. The path has been laid for us to trust God through our doubts and painful circumstances.

Just as Moses stepped out in faith to lead the Israelites through the wilderness, even when faced with uncertainty, we, too, are called to step forward into the unknown with unwavering faith. In the book of Joshua, we find the encouragement to be strong and courageous: "Be strong and courageous. Do not be afraid; do not be discouraged, for the Lord your God will be with you wherever you go." (Joshua 1:9, NIV)

The journey of faith is often met with obstacles and doubts, yet it's through these challenges that we have the opportunity to grow and show the world the strength of our convictions. Remember the words of Jesus in the Gospel of Matthew, "You are the light of the world. A town built on a hill cannot be hidden." (Matthew 5:14, NIV) Just as a city on a hill cannot go unnoticed, your courage and faith shine brightly for all to see.

As the apostle Paul wrote to Timothy, "For the Spirit God gave us does not make us timid, but gives us power, love, and self-discipline." (2 Timothy 1:7, NIV) Your convictions are fueled by the divine Spirit within you, empowering you to overcome fear and make a lasting impact.

So, as you journey forward in the radiance of your convictions, remember that your light has the potential to pierce through the darkness, just as the sun rises to bring forth a new day. Embrace the words of Jesus: "Let your light shine before others, that they may see your good deeds and glorify your Father in heaven." (Matthew 5:16, NIV)

Each step you take, every moment you live out your faith, contributes to the majestic tapestry of change woven by the Creator. Your boldness, courage, and unshakable faith are part of a greater story—one that transforms lives, illuminates the world, and reflects the eternal truth of God's love and purpose.

So, go forth with confidence, for you are an instrument of change, a beacon of hope, and a testament to the beauty of God's truth. Your journey is not just personal; it's a divine calling that ripples through time, leaving a legacy of faith and courage for generations to come.

Chapter 4

TRUST THE PROCESS

We often look at others lives and compare ourselves to their lives. We often think that their lives are better than ours, but we didn't know that God's plan for us may be bigger or better. God love to make his people out of nothing; this is very common when we walk with the Lord. We can see how God transformed Joseph's life using his brothers; there is such a thing as "The timing of God".

The Bible, our spiritual compass, teaches us to "Trust in the Lord with all your heart and lean not on your own understanding; in all your ways submit to him, and he will make your paths straight" (Proverbs 3:5-6). This timeless wisdom reveals a profound truth: that God has a meticulously crafted plan for each of us, a plan that transcends our finite comprehension and temporal desires.

The Lord had called me to share my story, to be a living testimony to His miraculous work. I had walked through the fire, and I was here to show others that they could too.

I often spoke about the importance of authenticity in ministry. I didn't want to be a phony, someone who wore a mask of spirituality while harboring doubts and fears within. So, I embarked on a journey of self-discovery, a deep dive into my own soul.

I turned to my husband, a chaplain who had witnessed the depths of human suffering in his work at the hospital, for guidance. He reminded me that the Spirit of God resided within me, capable of lifting my soul from the depths of depression. It was a revelation – depression was not my true self; it was a product of the wounded soul seeking redemption.

I delved into the essence of the soul, understanding its role in our lives. It is the bridge between the spiritual and the material world, constantly striving to fulfill our earthly needs and desires. But the enemy of our soul had been at work long before our physical existence.

The battle of depression and suicidal thoughts was not against flesh and blood in my life, but against powers and principalities that sought to hinder my destiny. But the Lord gave me a powerful revelation. I understood that my mess would eventually become The Message. As a powerful instrument in His service, He was tunning in me a sound of victory, even in the mist of my hopelessness all so I could tell to the people I minister to how he got me through.

Depression had been a constant companion throughout my life. Not only that, I also was born into a troubled family entangled in witchcraft and Catholicism, I had grown up feeling unloved and rejected. My parents' constant criticism against my physical appearance had left scars that I carried for years. For years I wore wigs, feeling completely naked without them.

But I had a revelation – I wasn't born to impress anyone but my Heavenly Father. I was fearfully and wonderfully made, with my unique features and qualities designed by God Himself. It was time to break free from societal pressures and expectations. If my Father in heaven had given me curly, kinky hair, who was I to question His divine choice?

The world bombards us with beauty standards, dictating how we should look and present ourselves. Makeup tutorials and contouring techniques seemed to be the norm, but I am ready to challenge that narrative. One day

I stood before my congregation, boldly declaring that I was fearfully and wonderfully made with my curly hair, and I would serve the Lord with confidence, unapologetically myself.

We need to understand that our existence was not a result of our parents' desires but a divine plan. We were sent into this world with a purpose, even if we didn't fully comprehend it. My own journey had brought me from a place of self-doubt and depression to a place of empowerment and purpose.

I continued to share my personal testimony and the journey I had undertaken to break free from the strongholds that had held me captive for so long. The devil had whispered lies into my ears, convincing me that I needed to conform to the world's standards to be accepted. But I had learned that true acceptance came from God alone.

In the darkest moments of my detox journey, I turned to faith as my anchor. I had to trust that there was a purpose behind my pain. I relied on the Word of God and prayer to find strength when my body and mind were in turmoil. It was a transformative experience that reshaped my perspective on life and healing.

The process of trust and transformation didn't end with detoxification or the reawakening of my soul. It was an ongoing journey of self-discovery, redemption, and growth. Today I reflect on how my faith, perseverance, and the unwavering belief in God's promises led me to a life of purpose, sobriety, and fulfillment.

Let us not judge an expert maestro before his work is finished, even though at first it may just be meaningless scribbles. Likewise, our life is like a canvas before God, and He is The Great Artist. It is never too late for God; He is outside of time itself. He operates on eternity clock and schedule.

When you are sad, put hope in God, He has not yet finish with you. Remember that the Maestro also paints our lives not only with bright paint, but also with dark/black paint. God didn't promise that our life will always be smooth like bright paint if we follow Him.

God wants to make each of us really enter into His plan, even in us Romans 8:28 says that God cooperates in all things, meaning this also includes both good things and bad things, for both of them bring goodness in our lives.

Sometimes there are also some things that are not in line with our thoughts. Why does the good we do turn out to be a disaster, just like the goodness of Moses which turns into a disaster in Acts 7: 23-24. Remember that God is not finished. Commitment to stick to God in all matters is still the best choice, even though all roads may be closed, and problems is all we face.

Romans 8:28 says" We know now that all things work together for good to those who love Him, that is, to those who are called according to God's plan. The above verse is a promise of God's care to His loyal followers who love Him with all their hearts. Remember to correct your motivation in following God; do you really want Him or only His blessings?

I don't know how to solve every struggle that you are going through, but one thing that I know very well from the nature of our God. He always has a way to amaze us with His work.

There is no doubt at all in following God, He always does things that are difficult for us to predict but easily fascinate us. Consider the story of Joseph in the book of Genesis. Joseph was sold into slavery by his jealous brothers, wrongfully accused and imprisoned, but he never lost faith in God's plan. In the end, he became a powerful leader in Egypt, saving his family and the entire nation from famine. Joseph's story exemplifies the importance of perseverance and trust in the face of adversity, for God's plan for him was nothing short of miraculous.

We must remember that God's plan is tailored to our individual talents and strengths. Each of us possesses unique gifts, bestowed upon us by our Creator, and God's plan seeks to utilize these gifts for the greater good. The Apostle Paul eloquently describes this concept in 1 Corinthians 12:4-6, stating, "There are different kinds of gifts, but the same Spirit distributes them. There are different kinds of service, but the same Lord. There are different kinds of working, but in all of them and in everyone, it is the same God at work."

When we trust the process, we acknowledge that our gifts are not to be squandered or compared to others, but rather, they are to be nurtured and used to fulfill our unique purpose in God's divine plan. For as the parable of the talents in Matthew 25:14-30 teaches us, those who faithfully invest their talents will receive even greater blessings from the Master.

Moreover, trusting the process means embracing a deep and abiding faith that God's plan is for our ultimate good. Romans 8:28 reminds us, "And we know that in all things God works for the good of those who love him, who have been called according to his purpose." Even in the darkest of moments, we can find solace in the knowledge that God is working behind the scenes, orchestrating events for our benefit.

Trusting the process is not a passive act but an active surrender to God's will. It requires us to release our grip on control and trust in the guidance of the Divine. Proverbs 16:9 reminds us, "In their hearts, humans plan their course, but the Lord establishes their steps." Our plans may falter, but God's plan is steadfast and unwavering.

Trust in the process allows us to find peace and contentment in the present moment. Often, we become so fixated on future outcomes and desires that we forget to appreciate the beauty and blessings that surround us today. The Apostle Paul learned the secret of contentment in Philippians 4:11-13, stating, "I have learned to be content whatever the circumstances. I know what it is to be in need, and I know what it is to have plenty. I have learned the secret of being content in any and every situation."

Life may be filled with challenges, and the enemy may try to hinder your destiny, but if you trust in God's plan and embrace your true self, you can overcome anything.

I had come a long way from the broken, insecure woman I once was. Through faith and a deep understanding of my identity in Christ, I had found the strength to stand tall, proudly displaying my curly hair as a symbol of my unique beauty.

This book is a testament to the transformative power of faith and authenticity. It is a reminder that we are all fearfully and wonderfully made, and our true purpose is to serve the Lord with confidence, unburdened by the expectations of the world. Trust the process, for God is with you every step of the way.

Chapter 5

LET YOUR FAITH BE FIRMED

One of the most common words we hear in any religious context is "faith". But the word is not a religious exclusivity. In the most different scenarios, we hear expressions such as "you have to have faith", "I put faith in this,"

At first, the concept seems simple; after all, faith is believing a in something, even when it seems impossible, right?

But what does this little word, which has such a huge impact on people's lives, actually mean? Is this really the definition given by the Holy Scriptures?

The dictionary defines faith as "belief, devotion, or belief in someone or something, especially for something that is not accompanied by logical evidence." Others define faith as "belief in and devotion to God." The Bible has a lot to say about faith and how important it is. In fact, it is so important that without faith, it is impossible to have a place with God. It is impossible for us to please Him (Hebrews 11: 6). Faith is a person's belief in trusting God without ever seeing Him in person.

Faith is "the foundation of things hoped for and the evidence of things not seen" (Hebrews 11: 1); faith is the work of the soul by which we are certain of the existence and truth of something that is not in front of us, or invisible to the human senses. It is a practice of faith that enables us to grow in believing the great truths God is pleased to reveal. Paul states, "our life is by belief, not by sight" (II Cor. 5: 7).

True faith is a living faith, a faith that always reflects a heart full of joy, graceful and praising God at all times. Gratitude to God is not a matter of how much we already have; thanking God is a matter of the attitude of the heart that has been changed by God. Thanking God is not because you have gained something, but thanks to God because we have a right relationship with God and understand why we bring our gratitude to Him.

There may be some moments in life that we think about stopping, leaving everything aside to be without the strength to fight. It seems that God has forgotten everything he promised you. Anguish in your heart. You don't see a solution anymore. With tears in your eyes, you can't smile anymore. Afraid of what's still there to come, if all this discouraged you and made you stop dreaming. The first solution is to cry out to the mighty God who will never abandon you. Cry out to your Creator; he understands your pain; cry out to the Father, the first one who loved you.

Don't think about leaving everything when Jesus already gave everything for you. It is worth resisting in the midst of the test; it is worth going through the desert when we are only accompanied by God, our happiness does not depend on people nor on what we have; it depends only on God because He will not give something you can't bear, and never take anything away from you if you really need it to survive.

Our adverse circumstances are not bigger than God when you understand that He is the one who will give you victory.

Many stories in the Bible tell of how great things are realized through faith. By faith, Moses parted the waters of the Red Sea (Hebrews 11:29). Noah built an ark and saved his family from the flood (Read Hebrews 11: 7). Elijah called fire from heaven (1 Kings 18: 17–40). "It was by faith that Sarah also, despite her advanced age, was able to have a seed, because she considered the author of the promise faithful" (Heb 11:11).

Faith makes us persevere in the promises of God, which may even delay, but does not fail, because with God nothing is impossible. Also, "it was by faith that the walls of Jericho fell, after a siege of seven days" (Hebrews 11,30). The sea was calmed, visions were opened, and prayers were answered, all through the power of faith. As we carefully study the scriptures, we learn that faith is a strong belief in truth in our souls that motivates us to do good. This leads us to ask: in whom should we believe?

A person of faith can see the extraordinary happen in the ordinary, which leads to a glimpse of what is not seen. If you have faith, you will perceive a possibility spring up out of the impossible. Faith is a mindset, like a pair of glasses you put on to connect to your reality from another perspective.

Faith is a way of pleasing God. Through faith, the invisible becomes visible, you receive strength, and you do what seems difficult because your actions are sustained outside of your natural ability. Through faith, you receive grace, which helps you in areas where you used to struggle before; faith makes life easier.

We can be inspired by a lot of biblical stories.

- God promised Abraham and Sarah a son; with faith, they had to wait 25 years to have him.
- God promised Noah that there would be a flood, but it took a long time to happen. With faith, Noah had to wait 120 years while building the wooden ark before God's words were fulfilled. He preached that there were going to be a flood at a time when no one had seen what rain looked like! It had never rained on earth before the flood.
- With faith, Jacob had to wait for 14 years to have the wife of his choice.
- The Israelites had to wait 430 years in Egypt before returning to the promised land.
- With faith, Ruth had to wait patiently before God provided Boaz to marry her.

- With faith, the woman who was bleeding profusely had to wait 12 years to be healed by touching Jesus' robe. She made her way through a pressing crowd who could have her killed, just because she beleived that Jesus could heal her.

Faith is what keeps you in the presence of God. It's the legal tender of exchange between you and God. When God sees you coming from afar, He watches to see what's in your hands. If He finds that faith is missing, you lose your audience and favor with Him. So, before you begin asking how much longer you must wait, you may as well want to make sure you have faith in your hands first. Without faith, it's honestly a waste of time trying to get anything from God. The value of faith cannot be exchanged. Faith is not just a currency of exchange to get what we want. It is a posture, an attitude that says: "My hope is beyond what I see, beyond what I experience and beyond what may come".

Jesus Himself spoke (John 20:29), "Blessed are those who do not see, yet believe". Job had a posture of faith. The kind of faith which dictated his actions and decisions in the most devastating circumstance he faced. Job refused to curse God.

Chapter 7

GIVE IT TO GOD

To surrender to God is another way of telling God that we're not big enough to deal with our worries, and He has to take over. When we finally let go, we give God room to wield his mighty arm in our lives. When our hands are weak and tired, God's hands are strong and mighty!

Giving it to God may seem frustrating at first, but our surrender will bring us freedom. When we let go, we give God a clean slate to do His mighty work in our lives.

You can give it to God when problems set in, when you are planning your wedding, when disappointment arises, when you are worried about your future. When there is a disturbance that you feel that makes the heart uneasy, when worries are not resolved, when your marriage is not going smoothly. A disease that hasn't been healed yet, give it to God. Maybe the sad feeling of losing a loved one. Maybe you have difficulty in achieving your personal goal. Financial hardship? The only person who can bless you abundantly is God; give it to Him.

All of these can make joy disappear and reduce your enthusiasm for life. For that, let's come to God. We can confidently rely on the power of God. God is willing to calm the wave of our struggle, or rather, He gives us the strength to face the struggle. Whatever challenges you are facing, the first solution is to pray that He will give you His peace that is "beyond all understanding" (Phil. 4:7).

What do Jesus, Job, Joseph, David, and Joshua have in common? They all went through great suffering, were persecuted, and experienced pain and tribulation. They had to go through situations of extreme complexity to reach their true blessing. Are the problems you have bigger than the ones they had to deal with? They understood that the first solution is to trust God and to give everything to him.

How about when along the way, those faith characters were mocked and despise by their own because of what they believed? Betrayed and abandoned in the mist of their season of waiting for the promise of God. They had to go through their dry and painful valley with only the help of God! Just like you and I, they were also tempted, and in some cases, they were afraid.

In Matthew 8:1-4 tells us a story about a man covered with leprosy.

It is important to note what Luke says about this man when he describes him in his Gospel. Luke records that, he was not a mere leper with only a blemish or two on his body. No! The evangelist reports that this man was covered with leprosy! (Luke 5:12). He had already reached his most advanced stage; his scent was the scent of death.

He was certainly missing parts of his body; his hands could no longer grasp anything, his gait was stumbling and staggering, his hoarse voice emitted ghastly sounds, and his odor was like that of a decomposing body. The only thing left for him was to wait for death, living on alms and the kindness of his fellow humans.

The man with leprosy no longer feared the mark of infamy and shame that separated him from his countrymen, for he had received faith from God, a faith that led him to trust and seek Jesus, believing that in Him he would surely find the solution to his problem. With faith and desperation, having nothing to lose, he approached Jesus, who did not despise him.

In worshiping the Son of God, that leper had placed his trust in Him, recognizing that Jesus was the only one to whom he should bow reverently and find his much-needed healing.

So, he humbly turned to Jesus and made a supplication to him, saying: "Lord, if you are willing, you can make me clean". This was his great yearning! His soul's greatest desire! The reverent trust and acknowledgment through his worship of Christ led him to beseech him that his leprosy might be cleansed.

Long story short, this story teaches us that whatever you are going through or facing, whether in your marriage, relationship, financial barrenness, womb barrenness, finding a dream job, or health issue, when you put your faith in God and make Him your first solution, He will supernaturally take care of all your worries.

Chapter 8

GOD IS ALWAYS WITH YOU.

Is it possible to follow God and progress in the secular world at the same time? Almost all Christians face this question on a daily basis in their workplaces, and many find the answer so difficult that it would be easier to give up. Daniel, the main character in the book of Daniel, faces this question under dire circumstances. Being exiled from Jerusalem when the Babylonian empire conquers God's people, he must live his life in an environment hostile to the Most High. Still, circumstances lead him to a position where he has a great opportunity in the service of the king of Babylon.

Daniel, a man of faith, openly prayed as usual, and kept his devotion to God intact, even though he knew he would be put in the lion's den. He is a man of faith. Daniel's life was full of trials. Certainly, Daniel's episode in the lions' den teaches us about the sovereignty of God, who later elevated Him to a leader in Babylon. This story shows how God is in control of all things down to the smallest detail. Nothing escapes the control of the God of Israel; He is the Lord of History.

Faith is a way of approaching God and an indispensable element for anyone who wants to achieve something new. Faith in God makes a person stronger and able to withstand the difficulties and adversities of life, thus equipping him to live a life that pleases the Lord.

When our faith in God is increased through the teachings written in the Bible, we can see much more than what is true and natural. It is through faith that we see the supernatural of God in action.

Our God has absolute power over everything and everyone. He controls nature, kingdoms, kings, and the entire Universe. He who opened the sea for the people of Israel to pass through is the same one who caused the walls of Jericho to crumble, preserved the prophet Jonah in the belly of a great fish, delivered three of his servants from death in a fiery furnace and closed the mouth of the lions in that pit.

Such a display of power made even that pagan king officially recognize the greatness of God. He made a decree saying that the God of Daniel is the living and everlasting God, whose kingdom is indestructible, and his dominion unquenchable. The pagan king declared that God delivers, saves, and performs signs and wonders in heaven and on earth. It was He who delivered Daniel from the power of the lions (Daniel 6:27). Otherwise, the king's understanding of God was very limited.

As I'm saying, Daniel knew that he was living in harmony according to God's will, and that he had done nothing to justify his condemnation. Because Daniel trusted in God, He sent His angel to close the lions' mouths. Daniel was aware of God's promises (Psalm 46:1; Psalm 34:7).

Then, all the men who brought charges against Daniel, with their families, were thrown into the lions' den. Before they reached the bottom of the pit, the lions took hold of them (Daniel 6:24). These men, who tried to liquidate Daniel, did so even though they knew of the innocence of God's prophet and the excellent record of his life.

From Daniel's story, we learned from Daniel to have faith and be brave in the most extreme situations. We can also learn that God cares about the day-to-day issues of our lives. The book of Daniel presents a hopeful picture of how God's people can survive and even thrive in a hostile environment through faithfully abiding in God. According to the book of Daniel, God has a deep interest in the daily lives of individuals and societies in a broken world. God intervenes directly in everyday life and also gives Daniel miraculous gifts that make it possible for him to thrive under an oppressive regime.

With unwavering faith and unyielding courage, Daniel's life serves as a beacon of inspiration for us all. His story teaches us that the pursuit of godliness doesn't have to be separate from worldly endeavors. It's possible to follow God's path while excelling in the secular world, and Daniel's life exemplifies this truth. Yet the days are coming, and they are already upon us when the New World Order will legally persecute the Christian faith in America for all eyes to see! Satan will soon have a table set for himself, on which he will satisfy his thirst for the blood of the true followers of Christ. Serious persecution is coming Church, brace yourself! It is already happening everywhere else on the planet!

In the face of trials, challenges, and even life-threatening situations, Daniel's trust in God never wavered. He remained steadfast, knowing that God's presence was always with him. The lions' den became a testament to God's ultimate sovereignty and ability to protect those who put their faith in Him.

Just as Daniel found strength through his faith, so can we. The challenges we encounter in our daily lives might not involve literal lions, but they can be just as intimidating. Remember that the same God who shut the mouths of the lions is the one who guides and guards us through our struggles. When we cultivate a deep and genuine relationship with God, our faith becomes an unbreakable shield against adversity.

Daniel's story reminds us that even in the darkest of circumstances, God's light can shine brightly. His favor and blessings can propel us forward in ways we can't fathom. As we strive to integrate our faith with our secular pursuits, let us take Daniel's example to heart. Let us be people of unshakeable faith, unwavering integrity, and relentless determination to put God first.

Just as God empowered Daniel to prosper in Babylon, He will empower us to prosper in our own fields of endeavor. Our faith will guide us, our actions will speak volumes, and our commitment to God will fuel our success. So, amid life's challenges and opportunities, remember that God is always with you, just as He was with Daniel. Embrace the journey, embrace the challenges, as they are the mark of a true believer in the Lord Jesus Christ. Like Daniel's, your story can be a testament to the incredible power of God's presence in your life.

Chapter 9

PATIENCE IS OF THE ESSENCE

Therefore, I am content with weaknesses, insults, troubles, persecutions, and difficulties for the sake of Christ, for whenever I am weak, then I am strong. 2 Corinthians 12:10

The Bible tells the story of a wonderful woman named Hannah. She was a kind, sweet and calm woman. However, even with these qualities, she had a painful life. Hannah's story is very similar to that of many women, but just as God turned her sadness into joy, He can do the same for you. I hope the story of this woman brings you hope.

The foundation of God's word for the theme of the story of Hannah in the Bible is taken from 1 Samuel 2: 1-2. Outside of the first two chapters of 1 Samuel, she is never mentioned in the Bible again. The writer of the book of Samuel, under the guidance, direction, and inspiration of the Holy Spirit, wrote: "Then Hannah prayed, and said, my heart shall rejoice because the LORD hath exalted the horn of my strength; My mouth scoffs at my enemies, for I rejoice in your help. There is no one as holy as our Lord. Because there is no one but you, and there is no rock like our God."

The story of Hannah in the Bible is one that inspires and motivates everyone who reads and studies it. There are many important and valuable lessons from the story of Hannah in the Bible. Her story teaches us to put God first in everything we do, how to let go and trust God regardless of our circumstances or situation, how to let Him direct our way, and how to trust His process when we are being tested.

The story of Hannah in the Bible should be a source of reflection for every person of God. What we can learn from this story is that abilities don't come from anywhere but from God.

As humans, we all experience ups and downs in life. There are times when we are at the peak of glory, but there are also times when life's problems take us into the valley of darkness. What is the role of faith for us? Maybe it's easier to have faith when things are going well. But what about when we experience problems and failures? Is faith still easy for us to echo?

The opposite of having faith in God is when we begin to do everything according to our will. We stop doing things thinking that there is a Creator who loves us, and we start performing our actions thinking only of solving our problems as quickly as possible.

The Bible says that Hannah and Peninah were wives of the same man named Elkanah. At that time, polygamy was tolerated, and a woman's worth was measured by the number of children she had. Peninah had children, and Hannah didn't; God has made her sterile. The Bible says that God has closed her womb."(1 Samuel 1: 5). As the years went by, and Hannah remained childless, her suffering increased; she was downcast by society due to her being infertile, which caused her to have low self-esteem, and her desire to be a mother increased daily.

But that was impossible because "the Lord had done this; He closed Hannah's womb." One may ask, "Why does He allow our suffering and humiliation?"

As we look at Hannah's life, we will see that our desire is often in accordance with God's will. *(John 15:7)* *"If we abide in me and my words abide in you, you will ask whatever our heart desires and it shall be done."* But His time is not our time; we must wait on the timing of God. In addition to the pain of being infertile, Hannah suffered from her rival Peninah, who had children, while Hannah did not. But despite all that was happening to Hannah, her husband loved her very much.

Once, at the house of Shiloh to worship the Lord, Elkanah, Hannah's husband saw Hannah crying and asked, "Hannah, why are you crying? Why don't you eat? Why is your heart sick? Am I not better than ten children?" (1Sam 1: 8) He really wanted to revive her, but there are certain pains that you are going through no one can cure, but God. Only God could comfort the heart of that woman who dreamed of holding a son of her own. After Hannah heard her husband ask if he was "no better than ten children," I can only imagine that she was so sad and got up and went to the temple to pray and pour out her heart before God. Yes, she went to worship the Lord and prayed her heart out. "How many times have we gone through terrible storms, and yet we still don't pray?" we leave the Gospel once and for all. It is because we often do not believe that God can give us the solution! The Bible says that Hannah prayed and wept with the bitterness of her soul because she was deeply shaken and trusted that God could work a miracle in her life. While she asked for a son, she made a vow with the Lord. See what she said:

"Lord of Hosts! If you look kindly at the affliction of your handmaid and remember me and your handmaid, do not forget but give your handmaid a son. I will give him to the Lord all the days of his life, and over his head will not pass a razor. "(1 Samuel 1:11)

Realize that this vow that Hannah took was not easy. She would conse-crate her son to God every day. But she said that because God was already putting in her heart a dream of having something more valuable than just a son. Likewise, when we go through great trials and tribulations, we often can see God working in our hearts, making our dreams bigger, and the higher the price is, the greater our reward will be from God. While Hannah con-tinued in the temple weeping in the presence of God, the Bible says that she prayed silently and moved only her lips. With that, the temple priest named Eli was passing by and saw her in that state. At the same moment, he scolded her because he thought she was drunk. Hannah, however, answered him very calmly:

"No, my lord, I am a woman troubled in spirit, neither wine nor strong drink has I been drinking, but I have poured out my soul before the Lord" (1 Samuel 1:15).

From there, the picture of Hannah's life changed. She left the temple happy and full of certainty in her heart that her life would change. The Bible says that she" went on her way, and ate, and her countenance was no longer sad" (1 Samuel 1:18). Hannah believed that God had heard her prayer, and with that, her sad face changed. She was at peace, for she knew that God would give her the son she dreamed of so much.

God is great and merciful; notice that it was God who led Israel into the wilderness. In the same way, each of us, before reaching his "Promised Land," must pass through the desert the way Hannah did. Our God does not send storms or diseases with the sole purpose to afflict us; He allows certain events in our lives to test us to know if we remain faithful and firm in the faith. He expects us to prove to him by our attitude and our faithfulness despite the difficulties.

This is the example we must follow! When we pray to God in faith and put all our problems before Him, we must change our countenance and let others see in us the brilliance that comes from a trusting heart in God!

Know that God has great rewards for us if we stay strong and pass the test. He will uplift you, promote you, and lead you to the Promised Land. James 1:12 says, Blessed is the man who patiently endures temptation; for after being tried, he will receive the crown of life, which the Lord has promised to those who love him.

Hannah's faith in the Lord brought her a miracle! She eventually had a son whom she named Samuel and was faithful to what she had promised God. She prepared the boy to serve the Lord for a lifetime. He later became one of the most exemplary leaders in the history of God's people.

God's promises may take some time. But do not lose faith. God's timing is key. The baby did not arrive on Hannah's time, but it was the perfect time.

God's timing was imperative because Samuel was destined to play an essential role in the transition of command between the time of the judges and the eventual establishment of the kingship for the Israelites.

Whenever your mind is troubled and bitter by the fear of uncertainty, do not let fear overwhelm you. Whenever you are afraid of something, say this to yourself. The Lord is my light and my salvation; whom shall I fear? The Lord is the strength of my life; of whom shall I be afraid, Psalm 27:1

God says *in* 2 Corinthians 12: 9-10: "My grace is enough for you, for my power is made perfect in weakness." So then, I will boast most gladly about my weaknesses so that the power of Christ may reside in me. 12:10 Therefore I am content with weaknesses, with insults, with troubles, with persecutions and difficulties for the sake of Christ, for whenever I am weak, then I am strong."

Chapter 10

TRUSTING IN GOD'S TIMING

In today's instantaneous world, it is very difficult for us to find patience or even to be patient. Because the demand of the contemporary world is speed, everything must be fast; targets must be achieved quickly, work must be completed quickly, communication must be fast, and so on.

Often, our prayers are not answered immediately; we ask God for something, or even not at all. At times like this, I always think of two things. One, this is not the right time for God, or God wants to keep me away from wrong choices and the dangers that could happen if what I want so bad happens for me. I believe God always has the best plans and blessings for each of us personally.

Today, many Christians become lukewarm and bitter in the process of waiting for God's promises, waiting for answers to prayers, waiting for God's help, and relying on our own strength to get out of trouble, which causes things to get worse and even postpones the blessings that God wants to provide.

Revelation 5:6 "I saw the throne with the living creature and there was a Lamb standing, as if slaughtered having seven horns and seven eyes, which are the seven Spirit of God sent out into all the earth". Notice here that it is the Lamb that is sited on the throne, and it is slain. Out of all the imagery and symbols, given in the bible, to understand the things of the Spirit, the Lord chooses a slain lamb. This must be significant!

We are in the book of Revelation, after the cross and the triumph of resurrection after all! The Holy Spirit could have shown the asserted authority of the champion God raised from the dead. But He used the lamb, not a roaring lion. The lamb had a cutthroat. The lamb was slain yet standing on the throne. What type of animal is slain with a cutthroat and blood running is standing?

I mean, I grew up in Africa, I saw how we slaughter meat animals and how we process it. And I'm telling you after the knife has gone through the throat they can no longer stand! But this lamb right here in Revelation 5, stand as if slain. He's standing with the blood running with an open wound. And that is his place of authority!

Let's back up a little bit. We're going back to Luke 22. You know, the Passover lamb in a Jewish tradition needed to be a lamb that they were acquainted with. They did not just go get a lamb out of the market and bring it to God and say, here's my sacrifice. It was a lamb that had been with them in the house. It was a cute little pet that they learn to love, cherish, and take care of. Yet the God of the Israelites required that the lamb Passover be brought to him to be slain. What The Lord Jesus requires of you is not cheap! I am sorry for the popular Gospel which makes everything so easy. But one of the meanings if not the main significance of the word Holy from the Hebrew Kadosh is: different. Standing on its own singularity! God is Holy. His ways are not our ways.

Waiting is indeed not an easy thing to do. The more we want one thing, the harder it is to wait, and along the way, we lose faith in God, just like Judas Iscariot. His tale is one of urgency, of desires. Judas, one of the chosen disciples, walked alongside Jesus, sharing in His teachings, and witnessing miracles that defied comprehension. Yet, in the shadow of his heart, a whisper echoed, urging him to forsake God's pace and seize control.

Judas, swayed by impatience, sought to hasten the fulfillment of God's plan according to his own whims. In the Gospel of Matthew, it is recounted how he was lured by the glimmer of thirty pieces of silver, a paltry sum compared to the eternal riches of God's grace. "Then one of the Twelve—the one called Judas Iscariot—went to the chief priests and asked, 'What are you willing to give me if I deliver him over to you?'" (Matthew 26:14-15).

His actions were a tragic illustration of humanity's tendency to prioritize immediate desires over the divine orchestration of events. In the haste of his heart, Judas attempted to trade the Messiah for material gain, disregarding the wisdom of waiting on God's timing. His choices remain a solemn reminder that the allure of quick fixes and shortcuts can lead us astray from the path of righteousness.

In our modern age, this timeless lesson continues to resonate. Just as Judas sought to speed up the unfolding of God's plan, many individuals and even entire churches succumbed to the temptation to rush God's work. It is a paradox that in a world defined by rapidity and efficiency, we often fail to recognize that God's timetable transcends our comprehension. "But do not forget this one thing, dear friends: With the Lord, a day is like a thousand years, and a thousand years are like a day" (2 Peter 3:8).

This is a warning to the ministers of the end time. Humble yourself under the mighty hand of the Living God and let Him exult you in His time. There is a Luciferian manteau ready for you if you jump out of season! Lucifer became hasty, irreverent, and his pride led him down the path of eternal disgrace. He lusted for prestige, for a bigger stage and a crowd all to himself and that greed turn him into an enemy of God.

Do not serve God with a heart that has the flavors of Lucifer's heart! If you do you will lose you reward. Signs, wonders, miracles, having authority over the demonic and a big congregation doesn't qualify you to receive a reward from the Lord Jesus Christ at His return. Check Matthew 7:21! On the contrary these criteria will be abundant as the return of Jesus is approaching.

Satan is looking for those who desire such thing, and he will be successful at trapping them! Resist!

The digital age has only exacerbated this inclination, as instant gratification becomes the norm. We find ourselves, like Judas, seeking shortcuts to spiritual growth, demanding immediate answers to our prayers, and expecting swift solutions to our problems. Yet, in this haste, we risk missing the profound transformation that unfolds through patient reliance on God's perfect timing.

The story of Judas is not merely a cautionary tale; it is a call to introspection. What are we selling Jesus for in our lives? Is it the allure of success, the pursuit of wealth, or the trappings of worldly approval? In the rush to secure these transient treasures, are we sacrificing the eternal riches that only God can bestow?

It is in moments of stillness, in the quietude of waiting, that we learn to truly align our desires with God's will. Just as the psalmist reminds us, "Be still before the Lord and wait patiently for him; do not fret when people succeed in their ways when they carry out their wicked schemes" (Psalm 37:7). Our faith is tested not in the speed of our actions, but in the depth of our trust.

There is no instant fulfillment of promises and help; everything has a process, and we must be patient. Here is an excellent illustration of patience with God's time. This analogy can be found in James 5:7. Farmers are looking forward to the harvest. A good harvest is depending on three things. The first is hard work (perseverance), the second is patience (Faith and prayer), and the third is God's time. Never expect more if we don't apply these three things. It should also be noted that ancient farmers did not have a good irrigation system; they only relied on rain. They must wait for the rain; it is even said to be "autumn rain and spring rain." They had to rely on the sovereignty of the Lord of the harvest!

God's promises always require the right time, when God fulfils His promises, and for this, too, patience is needed. Therefore, it takes a process of patience to face problems and come out as winners. Do not run away from problems, and do not look for shortcuts for solutions, but wait until God assures us what we should do next; even our new characters will be formed, and of course, there are blessings. The promise that God has provided behind every problem.

If you are currently giving up, or maybe you have begun to lose patience waiting for God's time, or maybe you have decided to do something because you feel God has not answered your prayers, stop! Turn to Him, ask Him for strength and wisdom, and wait for His time. Patience is not an instant gift either by the way! but patience is the fruit of the spirit, which is formed when we practice obedience and wait for God's time. Read Isaiah 30: 18-19.

Chapter 11

THE ONLY ONE YOU CAN TRUST

Isaiah 26:3–4. "You, Lord, give true peace to those who depend on you, because they trust you. 4 So, trust the Lord always because he is our Rock forever." (NCV)

Life can be filled with uncertainties and challenges, such as personal setbacks, professional obstacles, relationship issues, or health concerns that often leave us feeling anxious and restless. However, Isaiah reminds us that when we depend on the Lord, we receive a peace that surpasses all understanding. Amid chaos, confusion, and turmoil, we can find solace in God's peace, draw strength from our faith, and remember the words of Isaiah.

Isaiah reminds us that when we place our trust in the Lord, we are granted a peace that transcends all understanding. It is a peace that soothes our anxious hearts and quiets our restless minds. In the midst of any uncertainty, we can find solace in knowing that God's peace is not a fleeting moment, but a constant presence that guards our hearts and minds.

Know that your faith is a wellspring of power within you. Trust in the divine plan that guides your steps, even when the path seems unclear. Have faith that every challenge you encounter is an opportunity for growth and transformation. Embrace the lessons embedded within each trial, for they will shape unwavering character and resilience within you.

Faith in Christ allows us to step out boldly, knowing that He is the foundation upon which our lives are built. A firm foundation that withstands the fiercest winds. Trust Him, dear reader, for His promises never fail.

When the weight of the world feels heavy upon your shoulders, remember that you were not meant to bear it all alone. Release your burdens into the hands of a higher power, trusting that the divine knows your heart's desires and will guide you toward the path of light and fulfillment.

In Christ, we find freedom and peace. We are no longer bound by the expectations or opinions of others. We are children of the Most High, liberated from the chains of fear and insecurity. We can confidently walk the path set before us, knowing that God's plans are perfect and purposeful. Embrace your freedom in Christ, for it empowers you to be the person He created you to be. Remember who you serve and pay Him allegiance until the end.

The world is heading to perilous times and your allegiance to The Most High God will be tested! When facing to societal pressure of the LGBTQ+, abortion, and all the garbage the New World Order is trying to pile on us, remember who your allegiance goes to! Resist! The Church of the living God is not called to pacificism, but we are called peace makers. There is a big difference! There can't be peace if there is not war! But our weapons of warfare are not carnal but strong through the Holy Spirit to bring down imaginations and everything which exalts itself against the knowledge of God! Read 2Corinthians 10:4. Look around and noticed the absolute rejection of anything Godly in our culture today! Stand on the Eternal Word of God and Stand for it too! Resist!

Chapter 13

CALL ON GOD

"And David and his men came to the city, and behold, it was burned with fire, and its wives, its sons, and its daughters had been taken captive. Then David and the people who were with him raised their voices and wept until there was no more strength in them to weep. Also, the two wives of David were taken captive: Ahinoah, the Jezreelite, and Abigail, the wife of Nabal, the Carmelite. David was very distressed because the people spoke of stoning him, because the souls of all the people were in bitterness, everyone because of his sons and daughters; yet David strengthened himself in the Lord his God. 1 Samuel 30:1-25

In the text, we see that David went to battle, but when he came back, his city was on fire, destroyed, but he got stronger because in adversity, you either get bitter or you get stronger. David knew the counsel of the Word, the counsel of purpose, of the design of God from Moses, from Job, from all the prophetic scriptures that they had before him, and the Bible says that at this time when everyone was distressed, he got strong because he knew the God of his fathers.

The Bible says he was very sad and very upset, but he didn't feel bitter. So, guard your heart from bitterness, because it defeats you, because what defeats you is not the circumstances outside, but the attitude of your heart inside. What do you do in times of adversity? Strengthen yourself in the Lord. Enter the presence of God, consider, hear the Word, and let the Holy Spirit speak to you; you will be strengthened. He will less likely bail you out by the way, but His strength will carry you through to victory.

People were so bitter that they could not resister anger. When emotions take over, it clouds reason. David needed to listen to God, to hear the direction of the Lord, and while the people were blaspheming, he strengthened himself in the Lord. In times of adversity, go to your prayer closet, bend your knees on the ground, and cry out to the Lord your God because He can reverse any situation. And He does not reverse the situation He will transform you through and out of it. Ask Him to give you discernment to navigate in the mist of the storm. "Those who know their God shall be strong and will carry out exploits." Daniel 11:32

David didn't look for the general or the colonel, but he looked for the priest because he didn't think of arms or strength, but he thought of God, he thought of faith, and he remembered the priest. But what about you? What do you remember in times of adversity? What goes through your head, or what is the first thought that comes? Who to turn to or where to go?

The word adversity disrespects difficult times, so it's saying that when you conquer, rejoice, but when you are in situations you wouldn't want to be in, consider it because you will grow. The word consider is the same thing as scrutinizing, understanding why, and growing.

The prophet Elijah, after he defeats all the Baal worshippers on Mount Carmel, God sets fire to the altar that he saturates with water. Right after seeing that powerful display of God, the next place Elijah finds himself is hiding under a tree, wishing to be dead. He was physically tired, emotionally exhausted, his life threatened.

He was experiencing fear, resentment, anger, loneliness, and worry; he wanted to die. The Bible says in James 5:17 that Elijah was a man just like us!

Elijah was a prisoner in the prison cell of depression; it's a place where we've all been. But Christ always gives us a way out.

Isaiah 43:18-19 vs. 18 Remember ye, not the former things, neither consider the things of old. vs. 19 Behold, I will do a new thing; now it shall spring forth; shall ye not know it! I will even make a way in the wilderness and rivers in the desert.

When God allows His children to face problems, He promises that they will not exceed our strength, and He Himself will provide solutions so that we can endure them (1 Corinthians 10:13). When we fill our minds with God's promises, stress will no longer have a place there. We will be able to accept the situation with gratitude and be open to learning because we know that God can use everything to shape His children more and more like Him. He will even prepare us for greater things! Remember how Joseph was tempered through 13 years of hardship before he was made the second most powerful man in all of Egypt. Remember how Daniel's faith was put to the test while working under the rule of ungodly kings before he was finally given a high position over other officials in the kingdom?

Fear not when you feel like your surroundings are not working your way! God, the Creator, will continue to work to fulfil His plans in and through you.

Chapter 14

I CAN DO ALL THINGS THROUGH CHRIST

"I can do all things through Christ, because He [the one who] gives me strength." Philippians 4:13 (EBV)

In our journey through life, we often encounter challenges that test our limits and push us to the brink of despair. However, as believers, we are reminded of a powerful truth found in Philippians 4:13: "I can do all things through Christ, because He gives me strength." These words hold a profound message of empowerment and serve as a beacon of hope.

But what happens when you miss your job interview, or maybe a failed project, or maybe your dreams don't come true? Did you lack faith? Isn't God powerful enough? Or...did you take that verse out of context?

We must understand the meaning that Paul gives to this sentence. If we follow the logic of this passage, verse 13 offers us the reason why the apostle can experience contentment. Paul, how can you be satisfied and happy, despite all that you are going through? The answer he gives is simple and straightforward: "I can do all things through him who strengthens me," which is Christ. The "everything" that Paul is talking about here is therefore not an absolute to say that he can accomplish all the desires of his heart, **but rather that he can overcome all the situations that come his way,** be it poverty or abundance, failure, or success, married or single, Paul speaks of "all power" in very specific situations: physical distress and material abundance. If his circumstances changed, his joy and satisfaction in Christ would not change.

Do you have a project for the Lord, a dream that you want to accomplish and that seems impossible to achieve? You can do anything if Christ is in you! The lord is busy forming the image of who He is in the inside of you through those adverse circumstances. Jesus came and overcame evil as a man, to show us that it is POSSIBLE! It is possible to overcome if we let the Light of who He is shine within us as we are passing the valley of dire circumstances.

The end game is to produce eternal fruit in this temporal world. I realized through the years that The Lord is into the business of crafting works which can withstand fire and tribulation. And fire and tribulation would only decimate what is not authentically built in His Image, according to the design of His Will.

1Corinthians 3:13 talks about that fire which is coming to test all the works of those who call themselves Christian. Oh, what a glorious day for those who are busy manifesting Him at any cost. Those will shine like the sun. Make sure your obstacles, and negative circumstances draw you closer to Jesus Christ. Make sure that in the mist of the valley you go through, you still find grace to grasp some spiritual truth along the way. The spiritual truths that you are able to discern when you are in the mist of the fire, are nuggets of gold! Like the pieces to a puzzle, they will eventually form the bigger image. His Image, Character and His Nature will start to appear within you as you begin to know Him in the followship of His sufferance. Philippians 3:10

Remember the story of the tree Hebrew men thrown in the fire by a Pegan King because they refused to bow and worship him? In the book of Daniel, primary in the third chapter, we are told that the only thing that the furnace was able to burn was the ropes tied around their hands and feet. Yes, the fires the enemy of our salvation throws at us is only able to set us free from what bounds us and keep us from serving the True Living God! **If God is in the mist of your fire, then let it burn!** Find content in Him alone. You might not look good nor be the one on a stage looking all preppie and cute; but the Son of Man Himself when He carried his cross, look nothing like a dignify human being. Isiah 53:2-3

The truth of Philippians 4:13 breaks these chains, the chain of doubt and weakness. However, by acknowledging our dependence on Him, we tap into a supernatural source of strength that enables us to overcome any obstacle. The battles we face may seem insurmountable, but with Christ, we are equipped to face them head-on. His strength empowers us to conquer our fears, break free from self-imposed limitations, and achieve what we once deemed impossible.

Chapter 15

LET LOVE REIGN

In Matthew 22:37-39, Jesus responds to a question about the greatest commandment by saying, "Love the Lord your God with all your heart, all your soul, and all your mind. This is the first and most important command, and the second command is like the first: Love your neighbor as you love yourself."

Loving our neighbors and nurturing a strong relationship with God are essential aspects of leading a fulfilling and purposeful life. In today's fast-paced and interconnected world, it's easy to get caught up in our own struggles and forget the importance of extending love and kindness to those around us. But by examining our behavior towards our neighbors and deepening our connection with God, we can unlock a wellspring of love and compassion that will not only transform our own lives but also positively impact the lives of those we encounter.

As an individual facing challenging circumstances, it may feel daunting at times to love others wholeheartedly when we ourselves are struggling with our own faith. We may question our worthiness, our ability to give and receive love, and our capacity to make a difference in the lives of those around us. However, in these moments of doubt and uncertainty, it is important to remember that our struggles do not define us. They are merely a part of our journey, shaping us into the resilient and compassionate individuals we are becoming.

But remember that love starts with our relationship with God. When we pour out our love to Him, it overflows into our relationships with others and ourselves.

Proverbs 17:9 reminds us of the importance of forgiveness and covering offenses with love. Holding onto past hurts and grievances only separates us from those we care about. No matter what happened to us in the past, forgiveness and love can bring healing to broken relationships and cultivate an environment of peace for our children.

God's love is a wellspring of hope that never disappoints (Romans 5:5). Through the Holy Spirit, God pours His love into our hearts, giving us the strength and ability to love unconditionally. Embracing God's love enables us to extend it to ourselves and others, even in challenging circumstances.

Remember that our experiences, no matter how challenging, can be transformed into sources of strength and inspiration. Our stories have the power to uplift and empower others who may be going through similar struggles. By sharing our journeys and the lessons we have learned along the way, we can become beacons of hope and resilience to others.

Noticed the way several contemporary preachers selectively share about the authenticity of their walk nowadays. Fellow Ministers, the word of your testimony is what the People of God need to overcome their own battles. Testify! What did He bring you out of? How are you coping with the lows in your life? I completely understand that there are some situations difficult to talk about, or just simply too personal and the timing is premature. But we need to testify of the goodness of the Lord in what we go through. Our brother and sister would see God in a practical way, applicable in their own situations.

Luke 22:32 Jesus says something very interesting. "Simon Simon behold, Satan has demanded to sift you like wheat. But I have prayed for you that your faith will not fail. And when you have turned back, strengthen your brothers."

Peter had a very peculiar personality. He was impulsive and wavering. The same who took the sword and cut the ear of the temple guard the night Jesus Christ got arrested, is the same Peter after that went and sat with Jesus' enemies, warming itself with their fire. While Jesus was waiting for trial, the Same Peter denied Jesus. That nature is in us. Our human nature pulls us in contrary ways to the ways of God. Do not trust your humanity.

Paul said in Romans 7:19-25: "For the good that I would I do not: but the evil which I would not, that I do. Now if I do that I would not, it is no more I that do it, but sin that dwelleth in me. I find then a law, that, when I would do good, evil is present with me. For I delight in the law of God after the inward man: But I see another law in my members, warring against the law of my mind, and bringing me into captivity to the law of sin which is in my members. O wretched man that I am! who shall deliver me from the body of this death? I thank God through Jesus Christ our Lord. So then with the mind I myself serve the law of God; but with the flesh the law of sin."

In verse 32, Jesus says **"When you have turned back, Peter..."** I paraphrase, when you finally are getting out of fighting with your humanity, your soul that is always pulling you down... when you turn back from the painful journey of discovering that you cannot do anything outside of Me. And when you turn back from the process expulsing unstable Simon, **"strengthen your brothers"**. It is foreseeing what Peter had to go through that Jesus announced way before all this turn of events, in John 1:42: "You are Simon the son of John. You shall be called Cephas" (which means Peter). Simon, like most of us needed to become Peter, which means the rock, in order to be entrusted with the work The Lord had for him to do.

Satan don't want us to work with each other. The enemy of the Church is working relentlessly to kill our love and care for each other. He is good at dismantling our unity by infusing suspicion and distrust. I think that is why Jesus prayed very eagerly for us to be one. We need each other! We need to trust each other with the burden we carry and share the wisdom we get from our battles. I want to trust and freely say to my fellow brothers and sister in Christ "I've been through that and his is how God got me through this."

Fellow ministers! Testify and exhort the People of God in authenticity. Do not come to Sunday service only to show the people how dignify you are or exercise vein spiritual demonstration of "power" by aimlessly laying hand on folks to slain them in the "spirit". Build the faith of the People of God. Let them leave your ministration with applicable understanding about the Word of God. We are living epistle! Jesus, our Master did not act like a super star! Let us follow His ways.

Chapter 16

BREAKING AWAY FROM HERD MENTALITY

Herd mentality refers to the tendency of individuals to conform to the opinions and actions of a larger group. This can be observed not only in secular society but also within religious communities, including modern churches. The allure of cultural relevance can lead modern churches to reinterpret or even disregard certain aspects of the Bible, ultimately distorting the fundamental tenets of the Christian faith.

Breaking away from the herd mentality is a bold and courageous decision. It involves the willingness to question popular beliefs, challenge societal norms, and stand firm in one's convictions. In an age where cultural relevance often takes precedence over foundational truths, the journey of rediscovering and adhering to the teachings of the Bible becomes even more paramount.

The allure of conformity, the desire to fit in, and the fear of standing alone can lead us down paths that may not align with our true values and beliefs.

However, the Bible provides us with timeless wisdom and guidance on how to break away from this mentality and live a life of purpose and authenticity.

The Apostle Peter urged believers to be diligent in their study, "like new-born babies, crave pure spiritual milk, so that by it you may grow up in your salvation." (1 Peter 2:2, NIV) Just as physical growth requires nourishment, spiritual growth necessitates a regular intake of God's Word.

Breaking away from this mentality requires a sincere desire to seek truth beyond popular opinion. For Christians, this involves a return to the unchanging Word of God – the Bible. The Apostle Paul, in his letter to the Romans, emphasized the significance of renewing one's mind and resisting conformity: "Do not conform to the pattern of this world, but be transformed by the renewing of your mind. Then you will be able to test and approve what God's will is—his good, pleasing and perfect will." (Romans 12:2, NIV)

From the very beginning, the Bible emphasizes the importance of being separate from the world's patterns. In the book of Exodus, God calls His people out of Egypt, urging them to be a holy nation, set apart for His purpose (Exodus 19:6). This separation wasn't just geographical; it was a call to a different mindset and lifestyle. This concept is echoed in the New Testament, where Paul encourages believers not to conform to the pattern of this world but to be transformed by the renewing of their minds (Romans 12:2). Here are some examples from the Bible.

The Story of Daniel

The story of Daniel in the Old Testament serves as a powerful example of someone who refused to succumb to herd mentality. When he and his friends were taken into captivity in Babylon, they were faced with pressure to conform to the king's ways. Yet, Daniel chose to stand firm in his faith and principles. He refused to eat the king's food, which would have violated Jewish dietary laws. Instead, he requested a diet that aligned with his beliefs. Through this bold stance, Daniel demonstrated his commitment to his faith and his willingness to break away from the herd (Daniel 1:8-16).

The Courage of Esther

The story of Esther reveals the transformative power of stepping out of the crowd and taking a stand for what is right. When Esther learned of a plot to annihilate her people, she faced a difficult decision. She could have remained silent, blending in with the palace life, but instead, she chose to use her position to save her people. Her famous declaration, "If I perish, I perish" (Esther 4:16), reflects her willingness to break away from societal norms and take a courageous stand for justice and righteousness.

The Unwavering Faith of Shadrach, Meshach, and Abednego

In the book of Daniel, we encounter another powerful story of individuals who resisted the pull of herd mentality. Shadrach, Meshach, and Abednego were thrown into a fiery furnace because they refused to bow down to the king's golden statue. Despite the threat to their lives, they declared their unwavering faith in God, saying, "Our God whom we serve is able to deliver us from the burning fiery furnace, and he will deliver us out of your hand, O king" (Daniel 3:17). Their faith and courage to stand alone, even in the face of death, serve as a timeless example of breaking away from the crowd and remaining steadfast in their beliefs.

The Ultimate Example: Jesus Christ

The ultimate example of breaking away from herd mentality is found in the life of Jesus Christ. Throughout His ministry, Jesus challenged the status quo, confronting religious hypocrisy and societal norms. He surrounded Himself with outcasts and sinners, showing that His kingdom was not of this world (John 18:36). His teachings emphasized humility, love, and self-sacrifice—values that often contradicted the prevailing attitudes of His time.

Breaking away from herd mentality requires courage and faith. It means placing our trust in God's promises rather than the opinions of others. The Bible assures us that God is with us in our journey to authenticity. "Be strong and courageous. Do not be afraid or terrified because of them, for the LORD your God goes with you; he will never leave you nor forsake you" (Deuteronomy 31:6).

Just as Joshua was commanded to meditate on the Book of the Law day and night (Joshua 1:8), let us immerse ourselves in the Word, seeking wisdom and discernment. As we break away from the allure of diluted doctrines, we stand on the brink of a spiritual revival, igniting a fire that spreads from heart to heart.

Remember, it is often the solitary footsteps that blaze the trail for others to follow. The Bible's pages are replete with instances of courageous individuals who chose the path less traveled: Noah, Abraham, Ruth, and countless others. Their stories remind us that greatness emerges when we dare to deviate from the familiar and embrace the extraordinary. So, with hearts anchored in faith and minds illuminated by Scripture, let us step forward boldly, breaking away from the herd to forge a legacy of authenticity, resilience, and unwavering devotion.

Chapter 17

THE SHIFT FROM CHRIST-CENTERED TO MAN-CENTERED GOSPEL

In the realm of faith and spirituality, miracles have always held a special place. They are the extraordinary events that defy the laws of nature, demonstrating the divine intervention of a higher power. For centuries, churches have been sanctuaries where believers gathered to witness and experience these remarkable occurrences. But, in recent times, there seems to be a noticeable decline in the frequency and authenticity of miracles within the walls of many churches. This raises a critical question: Why are miracles no longer happening as they once did? The answer, it seems, lies in a shift towards a man-centered gospel over a Christ-centered one.

The Bible, a timeless and divine source of wisdom, provides invaluable guidance on how to live a life centered on God's truth. The apostle Paul, in his letter to the Galatians, sternly warned against any alteration of the Gospel, proclaiming, "But even if we or an angel from heaven should preach to you a gospel contrary to the one we preached to you, let him be accursed"

(Galatians 1:8, ESV). This solemn declaration underscores the unwavering nature of the Gospel and the dire consequences of deviating from its foundational truths. This warning echoes across time, urging believers to stand strong in the face of deviations from the true Gospel.

The story of Paul, once known as Saul, is a testament to the power of transformation when one embraces the Christ-centered message. Saul was a fervent Pharisee who ardently pursued a man-centered gospel, one rooted in strict adherence to traditions and legalism. His zeal led him to persecute the very followers of Christ he would one day champion. However, destiny had other plans for him.

On that fateful journey to Damascus, Saul encountered the risen Christ, a divine revelation that shattered the walls of his man-centered worldview. This encounter was not just a mere change of heart but a radical transformation that would shape the course of history. Like Saul, we, too, stand at a crossroads, ready to cast aside the man-centered illusions that limit our potential and embrace the boundless love and grace offered by our Savior.

In the pursuit of cultural relevance, some of us have strayed from the Bible's teachings. Some churches have reshaped the Gospel message to cater to the desires of individuals, emphasizing self-improvement, success, and material gain. While these actions might attract more followers in the short term, they raise important questions about the integrity of the church's mission and the authenticity of the Gospel message.

Words from the Scriptures remind us that our focus should transcend worldly pursuits and center on eternal values. The words of Jesus in Matthew 6:33 serve as a powerful reminder: "But seek first the kingdom of God and his righteousness, and all these things will be added to you." This verse underscores the importance of prioritizing a relationship with God and aligning our lives with His will, trusting that He will provide for our needs.

As I was saying, Paul's letters to the early Christian communities reveal the profound shift that occurred within him. He discarded the weight of a man-centered understanding and championed the message of grace, sacrifice, and salvation through faith in Jesus Christ. His writings resound with the liberating truth that our salvation is not earned through human effort, but through an unwavering trust in the sacrifice made on our behalf. As he writes in Ephesians 2:8-9 (NIV), "For it is by grace you have been saved, through faith—and this is not from yourselves, it is the gift of God—not by works, so that no one can boast."

Paul's journey is an inspiration for us to realign our perspectives. The transition from man-centered to Christ-centered living is a path of profound significance. It compels us to reject the allure of worldly achievements and temporary gains, and instead, invest in the eternal riches of spiritual fulfill-ment. Just as Paul's heart was rekindled by the flames of divine purpose, we, too, are called to become ambassadors of Christ's love and redemption.

In Galatians 2:20 (NIV), Paul encapsulates the essence of this transfor-mation: "I have been crucified with Christ, and I no longer live, but Christ lives in me. The life I now live in the body, I live by faith in the Son of God, who loved me and gave himself for me." This verse resonates as a reminder that our old selves must die to allow Christ's transformative power to take root within us.

Paul's message extended beyond cultural or social barriers. He recognized that the grace of Christ is all-encompassing and available to both Jews and Gentiles alike. His dedication to spreading the gospel exemplifies the urgency of sharing the life-altering truth with every corner of the world. As we stand in the wake of his legacy, we are emboldened to break down the walls that divide us and to share the message of love, hope, and salvation.

Let the story of Saul's transformation into Paul echo in our hearts as a symphony of hope and redemption. It is a call to abandon the empty pursuits of a man-centered existence and to surrender to the grandeur of a Christ-centered life. As we navigate the complexities of our modern world, we are invited to embrace the wisdom of Colossians 3:2 (NIV): "Set your minds on things above, not on earthly things."

Just like Zacchaeus, a tax collector, Zacchaeus lived a life centered around wealth and personal gain. When he heard that Jesus was passing through his town, his curiosity led him to climb a tree to catch a glimpse of the Savior.

Jesus' choice to dine at Zacchaeus' house shocked the crowd, but this encounter transformed Zacchaeus' heart. In the face of societal scorn, he rejected the man-centered pursuit of wealth and status and committed to following Jesus. He pledged to give half his possessions to the poor and to repay those he had cheated fourfold. His actions demonstrated a clear departure from a self-centered gospel, emphasizing that salvation goes beyond personal gain.

Ultimately, the effectiveness and impact of a church's message should be measured not solely by the number of attendees or popularity, but by the depth of spiritual growth, community building, and positive impact on society that it fosters. Straying from the Bible's teachings for the sake of attracting a wider audience can compromise the church's role as a source of spiritual guidance and moral grounding specially facing the coming apostasy.

Chapter 18

UNANSWERED PRAYERS

There was a child named Jon. After his dad came home from work, he prayed loudly enough for everyone to hear throughout the house from his room. "God, please buy me a bicycle; God, please buy me a bicycle." It was too noisy, so his mother went to his room and talked. "Jon, God hears you even if you pray in a small voice." Then Jon answered. "I know, Mom, but this prayer is for Dad to hear." After hearing that story, his mother said that prayer is to God, not so that people can hear.

Some prayers that go unanswered, but not all, stem from God's incomprehensible respect for human freedom and His refusal to coerce. Some, but not all, have dark powers that fight against God's people.

In the Gospel of Matthew, Jesus imparts the significance of approaching prayer with the right heart: "And when you pray, do not heap up empty phrases as the Gentiles do, for they think that they will be heard for their many words. Do not be like them, for your Father knows what you need before you ask him" (Matthew 6:7-8, ESV). Many of us are like this; we pray with the wrong heart. We have redefined the historic Christian faith by turning away from the proper way of praying.

Jon's belief that a louder prayer would somehow make his request more effective resonates with the tendency many of us have to seek human validation in our spiritual practice. Yet, his mother's response - "Prayer is to God, not to ask people to listen" - serves as a reminder that prayer is not a performance for an audience, but an intimate conversation with God.

The Bible is replete with verses that underscore the transformative power of heartfelt, sincere prayer. In the Book of Psalms, David writes, "The Lord is near to all who call on him, to all who call on him in truth" (Psalm 145:18, ESV). This encapsulates the essence of what Kennedy's mother was trying to convey - that true prayer stems from heart that yields to the Lord demonstrating pure motives.

The fact that God hasn't seemingly said yes to your prayers doesn't signify the need to give up; rather, it presents an opportunity to strengthen your connection with the Him and purify your motives.

I find some comfort in the fact that the Bible itself contains many unanswered prayers. Although we can only speculate on the reasons why God did not answer a particular prayer, these biblical examples give us some useful clues:

After leading the Israelites through the wilderness for forty years, Moses implored God to let him cross the Jordan with the people before he died. God rejects his request as punishment for his past outbursts, which haunted and grieved Moses so much that he addressed the people four times in Deuteronomy and unleashed his wrath on them, accusing them of being rejected by God. In other cases, Moses made God "change his mind," but not this time.

King David sat on the ground for a week, refusing food, praying for the life of his newborn child to be spared. As a result of his painful sin, his prayer was answered: David and Bathsheba lost their baby. However, a later union resulted in the birth of Solomon, who would rule Israel in its heyday.

Four Old Testament characters — Moses, Job, Jonah, and Elijah — even prayed to die. Fortunately for them, God ignored their demands.

On several occasions, the Israelite army prayed to defeat their enemies, only to suffer humiliating defeats. Each such event led them to inward research. Did the Israelites act hastily against God's commandments? Hadn't one of the soldiers committed an act that violated the laws of war, something that had displeased God?

The prophet Habakkuk prayed for deliverance from Babylonian oppression; Jeremiah prayed that Jerusalem would not be destroyed. Neither of the two prophets' prayers was answered, and each of them struggled to explain why the people suffered defeat. "Thou hast covered thyself with a cloud, that our prayer should not pass through thee," laments the prophet in a book rightly called the "Lamentations".

I could also mention some of the misplaced prayers of the twelve disciples, such as fire falling from heaven on the Samaritan village. In one situation, the disciples proved incapable of performing miraculous healing, and they seemed taken by surprise by that failure. Jesus used that opportunity to rebuke their unbelief. Although the disciples had not received an answer to their prayer, it was clearly God's will that the boy be healed, which is seen later when Jesus does what they were not able to do.

The apostle Paul, in turn, had some prayers that were rejected: it is enough to read his fervent prayers for the churches, and then to look at the sad record of those churches to see how far they were from the ideal for which the apostle had prayed. In his most famous unanswered prayer, Paul fervently prays to the Lord three times to remove the "thorn from the flesh." In an answer that remains as a model for situations when our prayers are not heard, Paul leaves behind the disappointment of not receiving what he wanted and instead accepts what he has.

Despite their prayers that are answered, these Biblical icons keep their faith burning; they didn't turn away from the teachings of the Bible. Their stories remind us that doubt can be a stumbling block on our journey of faith.

Instead, we are called to remain steadfast in our belief and trust that God's plan is unfolding, even when it's not immediately evident.

The story of Abraham and Sarah exemplifies the importance of holding onto faith despite the passage of time. In Genesis 18:14 (NIV), God promises the elderly couple a son, even though Sarah was well beyond childbearing years. The verse states, "Is anything too hard for the Lord?" This rhetorical question serves as a powerful reminder that God's power knows no bounds. Abraham and Sarah's unwavering faith eventually led to the fulfillment of God's promise, showcasing that His timing is always perfect.

The challenges faced by modern churches in maintaining their adherence to Biblical teachings can be overcome through the example set by the early Christian community. Acts 2:42 (NIV) paints a vivid picture of their commitment: "They devoted themselves to the apostles' teaching and to fellowship, to the breaking of bread and to prayer." By prioritizing these foundational elements, churches can create a strong spiritual foundation that withstands the pressures of cultural shifts.

In times of uncertainty and doubt, it's essential to remember Isaiah 40:31 (NIV): "But those who hope in the Lord will renew their strength. They will soar on wings like eagles; they will run and not grow weary; they will walk and not be faint." This verse reminds us that our hope and trust in God's plan can provide the strength needed to endure challenges and setbacks. Just as eagles rise above storms, our faith enables us to rise above life's trials.

The journey to authentic faith is marked by challenges that test our patience, resilience, and perseverance. Unanswered prayers do not signify a lack of God's presence but rather an opportunity to strengthen our connection with Him. When that greater bound is established, our love for Him and understanding of His ways begin to reshape our desires. By anchoring ourselves in the scriptures and exemplifying unwavering faith, we can find solace in the knowledge how God's plan is unfolding in our circumstances, and He becomes our delight, even if the answers are not immediate. Psalms 37: 4-5

In the next chapter, we will treat some conditions that God established for our prayers to be answered. Let's drive on!

Chapter 19

DOES GOD ANSWER PRAYERS?

The short answer to this question is "Yes!" Of course, yes. There are biblical texts and real-life cases that show that God answers prayers. The Bible says: "He will execute the desire of those who fear Him, and He will hear their cry for help, and He will save them" (Psalm 145: 19). God has promised that when we ask for something that is in line with His will for our lives, He will give it to us (1 John 5: 14-15). However, one caveat should be added to this: we may not always like the answer.

We pray for many things - something good, something bad, and something that may be meaningless. But God listens to all our prayers, no matter what we ask (Matthew 7: 7). He does not ignore His children (Luke 18: 1-8). When we turn to Him, He promised to listen and answer (Matthew 6: 6). His answer may be yes or no or wait, not now. 1 John 5: 14-15). If we pray to the Lord and the prayer does not correspond to His will for us, then He is unlikely to give us what we want. God's wisdom is far superior to ours, and we must believe that His answer to our prayer is the best possible solution. John 14:13.

Our prayers should be focused on what glorifies Him and reflects His will, which we learn from the Bible (Luke 11: 2). Our prayers must correspond to His will for us. God's wisdom is far superior to ours, and we must believe that His answer to our prayer is the best possible solution. When God Says "Yes," The first two chapters of 1 Kings talk about Hannah asking God to give her a child. She could not accept what was considered a shame for a woman in Bible times. Hannah prayed so fervently that the priest, seeing her, thought she was drunk. But the Lord heard the woman's prayers and allowed her to give birth to a child.

Jesus said: "I will do whatever you ask in my name, so that the Father may be glorified through the Son" (John 14:13.) If you have prayed for something specific and God has given it to you, then you can be sure that it is His will for it. Nothing happens without His permission (Romans 8:28).

When God Says No (John 11) describes how Mary and Martha wanted Jesus to heal their dying brother, but He allowed him to die. Why did Christ say no to these grieving women who loved Him so much? Because He had such incredible plans for Lazarus that no one could even imagine. If you have prayed for something specific and God has given it to you, then you can be sure that it is His will for it. Proverbs 3:5 says, "Trust the Lord with all your heart and do not lean on your own understanding." When we receive a negative answer, we must believe that what we asked for was not God's will. Romans 8:25

Although, getting "No" as an answer might make us heartbroken. But, again, it is important to remember that God is omniscient; He knows the whole story. He knows all the possible results of every possible decision in every possible situation; we are not given this. He sees the "bigger picture"; we see only a partial smear. Again, when we receive a negative answer, we must believe that what we asked for was not God's will. When God says, "wait, not now."

Sometimes, hearing "wait" is even more difficult than hearing "no," because it means we must be patient (Romans 8:25). While waiting is difficult, we can be grateful that God is in control and trust that His timing will be perfect (Romans 12:12; Psalm 37: 7-9). God wants the best for us. He does not want us to experience suffering. Jeremiah 29:11 says: "After all, I know my intentions for you," declares the Lord, "intentions to bring you prosperity, and not trouble, to give you a future and hope." Be patient and know that He is your loving Father (Psalm 45:11). While waiting is difficult, we can be grateful that God is in control and trust that His timing will be perfect (Romans 12:12; Psalm 37: 7-9). Psalm 45:11). Philippians 4: 6, turning to God with your requests: "Do not be anxious about anything, but in everything, through prayer and petition, with gratitude open your requests to God." Then, when the Lord answers, be ready to accept His wisdom - whether you agree with His answer or not.

Now, for God to answer us, we are expected to meet certain conditions.

Conditions that God establishes.

- Pray in faith. Without faith, we cannot please God (Hebrews 11: 6), who alone can do the impossible (Luke 1:37). What is the use of praying without faith? John 16:24). He is the reason why we can approach the throne of grace. Believe—have full faith in God's love, mercy, and promises—and expect answers (Mark 11:24; Hebrews 10:22).
- Be humble and sincere. The Bible says: "Though the Lord is great, he cares for the humble, but he keeps his distance from the proud." (Psalm 138: 6).
- Persevere. Jesus gave this guarantee: "Keep asking, and it will be given unto you" (Luke 11: 9).
- Pray with a grateful heart, be extremely grateful to God and express thanksgiving and praise profusely (Philippians 4:6; Colossians 4:2).
- Be wholehearted, fervent, and passionate in prayer (James 5:16; Psalms 119:145; Hosea 7:14).
- Ask God to guide and inspire you with His Holy Spirit (Romans 8:14-15, Romans 8:26-27; John 14:26).

- Pray with a righteous heart (Matthew 7:11). We do not always understand what is good, but God knows this and strives to give His children what is best for them. Paul prayed three times for deliverance from grief, and each time, the Lord answered, "No." Why did a loving God refuse to heal the apostle? Because he had something better for him, namely a life by grace. Paul stopped praying for healing and began to rejoice in his weakness (2 Corinthians 12: 7-10).
- Pray for the necessary things (Philippians 4:19). The highest priority for God's kingdom is one of the conditions for prayer (Matthew 6:33). The promise is that God will satisfy all our needs, not all of our desires. There is a difference between the two.
- Pray constantly (Luke 18: 1). The Bible tells us to pray unceasingly (1 Thessalonians 5:17). One of the conditions for effective prayer is that we do not stop praying.

Godly, effective prayer has conditions, and the Lord invites us to pray. When should we pray? All the time and do according to His will.

What does it mean to pray according to the will of God? Praying in the will of God is praying for something that will glorify God and/or something that is clearly revealed in the Bible to be God's will for us. If we are praying for something that does not glorify God or is not in line with God's will for our lives, God will not give us what we ask for.

How can we know what God's will is? God promises to give us wisdom if we ask for it. James 1:5 says, "If any of you lacks wisdom, let him ask God, who gives freely to all and without reproach, and it will be given to him." Study what the Bible says about God's will for your life. The better we understand God's Word, the better we know what to pray for, and the more effective our prayer life will be.

Chapter 20

BE A PART OF THE FAITHFUL GENERATION

The great apostasy is already happening! There is an unwavering call for a generation that stands firm in faith, rooted in the unchanging truth of the Word of God. The faithful generation is not just a concept; it's a destiny waiting to be claimed. It's a path that requires dedication, persistence, and, above all, a heart turned toward the Creator.

Although, circumstances might occur along the way, but it is better we know that human life is inseparable from various events, obstacles, challenges, experiences, and opportunities. All of that could be used as a lesson for everyone to become a better person today. Experience is the best teacher, they say, who teaches many things to not fall into the same mistake a second time.

Many people are experiencing and going through a painful and tough phase of life. Life is like an endless drama, especially for those who are less grateful; they will consider that life is a heavy curse. In life, of course, we experience many unexpected things. Sometimes, we are tired and need life inspiration words to increase our enthusiasm. Sometimes, we don't realize how beautiful the Almighty designs life. Sad, happy, and disappointed are spices that make life more meaningful.

In life, a world of difference exists when it comes to our faith, where fear takes precedence over our ability to choose. As a human being, you are not wired to be controlled by your circumstances. You are wired to believe in God, thrive and grow, and become whatever you are meant to be.

For all these things to work well, you need the Holy Ghost, "The Holy Ghost can do for us physically, spiritually, emotionally, mentally, and intellectually what no man-made remedy can ever duplicate,"

God is your loving Father in heaven and wants to hear from you. You can approach Him through praying earnestly and persistently. To be part of a faithful generation is to be rooted in God's promises and unwavering in our trust. Hebrews 11:6 reminds us that "without faith, it is impossible to please Him, for whoever would draw near to God must believe that He exists and that He rewards those who seek Him."

Our prayers are not in vain; they are powerful instruments that shape our hearts and the world around us; as James 5:16 declares: "The prayer of a righteous person has great power as it is working." Prayer is not merely a request; it's a conversation with the Almighty. As you seek to be part of the faithful generation, remember the words of Jeremiah that says: "Then you will call on me and come and pray to me, and I will listen to you. You will seek me and find me when you seek me with all your heart." 29:12-13 (NIV).

To be part of the faithful generation is to stand upon a foundation that is unshakable – the historic Christian faith and the teachings of the Bible. The truths that have guided generations before you remain as relevant and powerful today as they were centuries ago. Hebrews 13:8 (NIV) reminds us: "Jesus Christ is the same yesterday and today and forever."

In a world that clamors for novelty, hold fast to the timeless truths of Scripture. Let your life be a testament to the consistency of God's promises and the transformative power of His Word. As Psalm 119:105 (NIV) proclaims, "Your word is a lamp for my feet, a light on my path." The faithful generation believes not in the limitations of man, but in the limitless power of God. It's a generation that recognizes that human strength can falter, but God's strength is perfected in weakness.

It is through a relationship that we can approach Him and pour out our soul, tell Him everything. God must be our greatest confidant, the most reliable and genuine, someone we know will never betray or give us bad advice, someone who, despite being perfect, does not condemn or judge us unjustly, but loves us and offers us his forgiveness.

The faithful generation does not retreat from the world. Instead, they engage with it, infusing every interaction with the light of Christ's teachings. They are not driven by a desire for personal recognition or temporary pleasures; their joy comes from aligning their lives with God's purpose. They stand firm amidst the world's challenges, and they refuse to step back from the world's complexities. Instead of retreating, they actively embrace it, imbuing every interaction with the illumination of Christ's lessons.

I want to be a part of the faithful generation. A people who persists in holding fast to the timeless truths of Scripture. Their lives are living testimonies to the enduring power of God's Word and the transformative impact of living according to His will. Through their faith, love, and dedication, they inspire others to embrace a life of purpose, guided by the unchanging light of God's eternal truth.

Chapter 21

EXAMINATE YOUR CONSCIENCE

"If we claim to be without sin, we are deceiving ourselves, and the truth is not in us." 1 John 1:8

I wonder, what does the word confess imply? What does one do when he confesses his/her sin to the Lord? The word 'confess' means "admit and acknowledge." Confessing our sins to the Lord shows that we recognize that we have failed him and need his forgiveness. Only through his forgiveness that we will be able to walk in the process of sanctification in our lives. It is only in confessing our sins that we will find mercy and help from God; as Proverbs 28:13 says, "He who covers his sins will not prosper, but he who confesses them and turns away will obtain mercy."

But why is it so important to confess our sins? Plain and simple because our prayer will not be heard by God. "If I see iniquity in my heart, the Lord will not hear me" (Psalm 66:18). But nowadays, confessing your sins is something people no longer want to do. Today, people often blame others for their sins and say, "It's not my fault!"

I will tell you a story of a man called Frederick the Great - the King of Prussia. He was visiting a prison and talking to each of the inmates. As he spoke to them, he heard endless reports of innocence, exploitation, and misunderstood motives. Of course, no one in that prison was guilty. All of them were innocently imprisoned. Finally, the king stopped in the cell of a convict who remained silent. Frederick said, "Well, I suppose you're an innocent victim, as other claims." "No sir," the prisoner said, "I am not. I am guilty, and I deserve my punishment." Turning to the director, Frederick said, "Quickly, get this man out of here before he gets corrupted by these other innocent people." Frederick the Great could not believe he had found an honest man.

What a great truth! We tend to say, "It's everyone's fault but not mine." But there will have to be a time in your life when you say, "I have sinned. I have committed this iniquity. I am the cause of my problem." The day you confess all your sins and turn to the Lord will be the day God changes your life. Repent, believe in the Lord Jesus, and be baptized, this is the way to salvation. Act 2:38

As we all know that sin separates us from God. When we disobey any of the commandments, we put up a wall between us and him. But the Bible provides a solution to this barrier: repentance aka turning away.

There is that worldly saying: "Too late to change", or "There is no point in changing". This type of silly language is enough to make us seem hesitant to make the decision to change.

But even so, in this life, it is never too late. You can do it now. It's never too late to start over. What are you waiting for? It's never too late to make changes and self-improvement.

If there is any, I beseech you to confess and ask for forgiveness today; don't postpone it until tomorrow. Tomorrow might be too late. Stop being lazy. Now is the time to make peace with the Lord Jesus Christ.

Chapter 22

OLD THINGS HAVE PASSED AWAY

2 Corinthians 5:17: "Therefore, if anyone is in Christ, he is a new creation; old things have passed away; behold, all things have become new." In Christ, we are transformed. As individuals who are going through a difficult time, it's easy to carry the weight of past mistakes, failures, and disappointments. But take heart, for God's love is greater than any burden you bear.

When we face adversity and challenges, it's natural to feel disheartened and even question the path we're on. The struggles we encounter might make us want to voice our complaints and grievances, seeking relief and understanding. However, we must remember that the journey of faith is not without its trials, and the way we respond to these trials speaks volumes about our character and our relationship with God.

In the face of difficulties, let's draw inspiration from the Biblical wisdom found in Romans 5:3-5: "Not only so, but we also glory in our sufferings, because we know that suffering produces perseverance; perseverance, character; and character, hope. Hope does not put us to shame because God's love has been poured out into our hearts through the Holy Spirit, who has been given to us." Just as gold is refined through fire, our faith is tested and strengthened through trials.

The thing is that you cannot escape your entire life from the past. You must face the present, live it, and move forward, knowing that God has something bigger for your life. But for some of us, instead of moving forward, we simply stay tied to the past, just like the people of Israel.

When the people of Israel remembered the food in Egypt, they were not thinking of all the beatings they received, the heat they suffered, and all the work they did. When they complained about what they didn't have, they selected the best memory from their past. They remembered a meal that wasn't even that good, which was leftovers, but they did it simply to stay tied to the past.

But as the wise scriptures remind us, in Philippians 3:13-14, "Brothers and sisters, I do not consider myself yet to have taken hold of it. But one thing I do: Forgetting what is behind and straining toward what is ahead, I press on toward the goal to win the prize for which God has called me heavenward in Christ Jesus."

Just as the Israelites clung to a distorted memory of their past, we too often hold onto the shadows of our former days. We let the weight of our past mistakes, hardships, and missed opportunities burden our spirits and obstruct our journey toward the promised land of God's purpose for us.

Yet, God's message is clear: Do not dwell on the past. The Almighty did not chastise them solely for their discontent but used their experience as a teaching moment. Just as a loving parent guides a child, the Creator disciplined the Israelites, not out of anger, but out of a deep desire for their spiritual evolution. For it is through trials and tribulations that true growth emerges, and so, a punishment was meted out.

Let us not be misguided by the word "punishment," for it was not retribution but rather an opportunity for transformation. The Israelites were assigned tasks that required dedication, perseverance, and faith. They were given a chance to shed their longing for the past and to embrace the challenges of the present, forging a path towards a brighter future.

In our lives, we, too, encounter moments of nostalgia that entice us to hold onto what was, even if it was fraught with difficulties. But let us remember the Israelites' journey as a mirror to our own struggles. Just as their complaints led to growth through disciplined tasks, our own challenges can be catalysts for our personal development.

When we find ourselves facing punishment for expressing our complaints, let us turn to 1 Peter 2:20: "But how is it to your credit if you receive a beating for doing wrong and endure it? But if you suffer for doing good and you endure it, this is commendable before God." Enduring hardships for the sake of righteousness is an act that resonates with the very essence of Christianity.

Just as the Israelites were led by a pillar of fire by night and a cloud by day, we are guided by God's unwavering presence. His promises are our sustenance, His grace our strength. We must trust that what lies ahead is greater than anything we leave behind. Even when the journey seems uncertain, we can take refuge in the assurance that the Lord's plans for us are plans of hope and prosperity.

So, when the urge to complain arises, let us turn our complaints into prayers, seeking God's guidance and strength to navigate the challenges before us. By embodying the virtues of patience, endurance, and unwavering faith, we not only honor our calling as Christians but also shine as beacons of light in a world that desperately needs the message of hope and transformation.

God has a new life for you; he has something greater for you. Remember that you were called to go from glory to glory, from triumph to triumph, from blessing to blessing. Declare today what Paul declared, *in Philippians 3:13-14 "one thing I do: forgetting what lies behind and straining toward what lies ahead, I press on toward the goal for the prize of the upward call of God in Christ Jesus."*

Chapter 23

UNLIMITED POSSIBILITIES, VICTORY AT LAST

"Ah! Our God, will you not execute your judgment against them? Because in us there is no strength to resist this great multitude that is coming against us, and we do not know what to do, but our eyes are on you." 2 Chronicles 20:12

King Jehoshaphat is one of the biblical characters I like to cite as an example of faith positioning.

Faced with the news that a large army was about to attack him, Jehoshaphat was afraid, but wasted no time: he went to seek the Lord and put all his people to do the same.

Of course, no one wants to face a threat of this level. Of course, we're not made of ice either; that is, when we receive terrible news or are simply in the middle of a sticky situation, we feel fear at first, but after the initial impact, we have other reaction options, and they will define the "next chapters" of our story.

The phrases that almost automatically come to our minds are: "Now what? I can't, I won't, I can't, no, no, no." Okay, we are all human, and we can make the mistake of looking at our limitations. However, having God with us, we cannot allow the lack of control to take over our lives and lead us to despair. Understand that taking a stand contrary to what the circumstances suggest involves trusting in God; it involves faith in His Word.

What biblical promises have you held on to? Where are your eyes set? Whichever direction you choose to look will create your victory or your failure.

There are always several possibilities for reaction when adversity is in front of us, but fixing our eyes on God is what will guarantee that, in the end, we will be saved. That's what King Jehoshaphat did, and he defeated a people enemy of his nation Israel.

Not only did King Jehoshaphat and other great men of God suffered adversities, but each one of them brought great victories to their lives, which are also our victories.

We see the life of Joseph: he was sold, his brothers rejected him, he spent time in jail, they accused him unfairly, and he was away from his family for a long time, but in the end, all the adversity that had been overturned in his life ended in an exceptional victory.

"Then Joseph said to his brothers: Come near to me now, and they came closer, then he said: I am your brother Joseph, the one you sold into Egypt. Now, do not be saddened nor regret that you sold me here; because, for the preservation of life, God sent me before you." (Genesis 45: 4-5 KJV)

What can we say about Esther, who was taken to the palace, separated from her only relative, Mordecai? But even adversity came to the palace: Haman the wicked, out of envy, made the king decree death to all the Jews, the race from which Esther came.

She exposes her life before the king, because if she was not called by her husband the king, the punishment was death, but she did not care, since what motivated Esther to move forward was to save her people. With all wisdom and in danger of losing his life, he confronts the king, and he has a great victory.

"All the king's servants and the people of the king's provinces know that any man or woman who enters the inner court to see the king without being called, there is only one law regarding him: he must die, except the one to whom the king extends the golden scepter, who will live; and I have not been called to see the king these thirty days. Go and gather all the Jews who are in Susa, and fast for me, and do not eat or drink for three days, night and day; I will also fast with my maids, and then I will go in to see the king, even if it is not according to the law; and if I perish, let me perish." (Esther 4:11, 16 KJV)

She suffered tremendous adversity, but having faced the king despite the edict, Esther had a great victory: The Jewish people were saved from being exterminated, and to this day, Purim is celebrated, a festival where every Jew gives thanks for life, and they remember everything that Queen Esther did to save them.

What about David? David was persecuted by Saul for reasons of envy. It was a time of peril, but by going through this adversity with perseverance and trust in God, he was victorious.

"I am afflicted and needy; from youth, I have borne your terrors; I have been fearful. Your wrath has passed over me, and your terrors oppress me. They have surrounded me like water continually; I have been surrounded by one. You have removed friend and companion from me, and you have put my acquaintances in darkness." (Psalm 88: 15-18 KJV)

Knowing that he was going to be king from a young age, he did not brag, but waited for God's timing. He spent many years running from Saul to protect his life, but in the end, when he was finally king, he became the best known and most victorious king of Israel.

As we can see in each of these stories, when adversity knocked on the door, God came out to meet them and gave them triumph over adversity.

"Do not lose, then, your confidence, which has a great reward; because patience is necessary for you, so that having done the will of God, you may obtain the promise." (Hebrews 10: 35-36 KJV)

"One thing I notice from these Biblical icons is that they kept the fire of their faith burning. They never defected from the way of God, and in the end, God answered all their prayers."

The lessons imparted by these biblical icons offer a vital reminder to today's faithful. Their stories emphasize the importance of staying true to the teachings of the Bible, ensuring that faith remains unwavering and robust. By studying their journeys, we can learn from their unwavering commitment to God's word, reinforcing our own spiritual foundations and preserving the authenticity of the Christian faith for future generations.

In a rapidly changing world, where societal norms and values can sometimes seem uncertain, the teachings of the Bible provide a steadfast anchor. They remind us of the importance of love, compassion, forgiveness, and humility, values that are essential for building strong, harmonious communities.

As we navigate the complexities of modern life, we need not turn away from the teachings of the Bible. Instead, we can draw upon the wisdom of these biblical icons to guide our actions and decisions, helping us lead more purposeful and virtuous lives. In doing so, we honor the enduring legacy of these iconic figures and the profound impact they have had on our collective consciousness.

Conclusion

The decline in biblical literacy is a complex challenge, partly stemming from shifting societal norms and values. It is crucial to acknowledge that the changing approach of certain churches towards biblical interpretation exacerbates this issue. To address this concern, churches must return to God's foundation, as underscored by 1 Corinthians 3:9-15. By building upon the solid rock of Christ and His teachings, congregations can ensure that their spiritual edifices remain strong and resilient against the storms of worldly influences. Through a renewed commitment to biblical literacy and interpretation, churches can once again flourish as beacons of truth, guiding believers toward a deeper understanding of God's Word and His divine plan.

In this soon ending world, where the forces of secularism and materialism often seem to hold sway, the church must stand as a firm and unwavering pillar of faith. The church should remain undefiled, entrusted with the timeless truths of Scripture, a repository of divine wisdom, and a sanctuary for the souls seeking relief in the embrace of faith. The Church of Christ, His body and His Bride must NEVER adapt to the shifting tides of societal culture but needs to anchor itself in the unchanging Word of God.

As we reflect upon the challenges and opportunities that lie ahead for the church, we must remember that the essence of our faith is rooted in a foundation that cannot be shaken. It is a foundation laid by the divine hand, built upon the cornerstone that is Jesus Christ. Just as a master builder carefully selects the materials for a lasting structure, so too must the church choose to build upon the solid rock of God's Word.

The call to rekindle biblical literacy and uphold the sanctity of Scripture is not a call to retreat into the past, but a call to embrace the timeless truths that have guided generations of believers. It is a call to engage with the Word of God in a way that is relevant to the challenges and questions of our time. It is a call to approach the Bible with reverence, humility, and a sincere desire to understand and apply its teachings.

The church's mission is not confined to the walls of its physical buildings. It extends to the far reaches of society, where the light of God's Word is needed most. It is a mission that requires a firm foundation, for only with a solid footing can the church effectively reach out to a world in need of hope and redemption.

The church is not defined by its traditions or its structures, but by YOU and I unwavering commitment to the Word of God. Stand firm in order to be rewarded!

I would like to consider the death of Steven. As he stood before the Sanhedrin, preaching boldly, he knew he was walking right into his demise. Nevertheless, he did it for those listening to him. He was so passionate about his Savior that he served the least of these, faced intense persecution, and ultimately gave his life for his Rabbi. He set the example for millions of Christians throughout history.

The Bible says that Stephen's court members gnashed their teeth and threw stones at him after accusing the religious officials of killing Jesus. As he was about to die, this man of God saw the heavens open and Jesus standing at the Father's right hand, welcoming him home in a manner consistent with the Holy Spirit's visible presence on him. In the New Testament, this is the only time Christ stands rather than sits, and He does it in honor of someone who loved Him enough to give his life.

If you stand up for God, He will stand up for you! Be like Stephen if you want to hear Jesus say, "Well done, good and faithful servant." Embrace widows, orphans, young people, and those in need. For the sake of the Gospel, be ready to live and die. I believe Christ will be standing at the end of your earthly days to welcome you home to heaven if you are willing to plant trees for tomorrow with your own blood. Do not fear the consequences of being a faithful follower of Christ. If you have faith, you will be rewarded in the end. Be brave and have faith, and God will be with you.